Dear Dr. Grams,

"I really liked your book, Breastfeeding ~~Success~~ ~~for~~ Working Mothers. Yours is the first book I've read with practical information. Everyone said that The Womanly Art of Breastfeeding was the best for nursing mothers, but I was disappointed because it never really said how to do it. Yours does that very well... Another thing I didn't like about The Womanly Art was that it implies that it is best for mothers to stay home with their families and not work. But you assume that women will want to continue working and do not need to feel guilty about it. That's a refreshing attitude."
  -M.A.R., New York

"Your book is absolutely wonderful. It's the best I've ever read. Even your outlook on problems gave me new hope for my own crisis... You really inform mothers of exactly what to do. Most books are so general they really don't tell how and why and what... Nursing three children, mostly all of what you have said and experienced is really true. I didn't work but you seemed so relaxed in your book about nursing and seemed to learn so much it really was a blessing to read."
  -K.S., California

"First, I want to congratulate you on a very informative, easy to read and delightful book. I just recently finished reading it and would like to purchase four: one for myself, a friend, my pediatricians for clientele use, and one for our local hospital... I would highly recommend this book for anyone planning to breastfeed."
  -T.D., North Carolina

"Please accept a bit thanks from lots of us 'nursing moms' in Tomahawk, Wisconsin. We've found a great deal of helpful, sound advice as well as encouragement and problem-solving."

"Your book is terrific! So many books on breastfeeding give me the impression that they were researched (to whatever extent) and then pieces of other people's thoughts were stacked up and typed together to make a "book." Not yours - it's really outstanding."
  -E.T., Pennsylvania

Breastfeeding Success for Working Mothers

Marilyn Grams, MD
cover and illustrations by Itoko Takeuchi

National Capital Resources, Inc.
Carson City, Nevada

Distributed by Achievement Press
Sheridan, Wyoming

Breastfeeding Success for Working Mothers

by Marilyn Grams, MD

Published by:
> National Capital Resources, Inc.
> 1000 East William Street, Suite 100
> Carson City, NV 89701, USA

Distributed by:
> Achievement Press
> P. O. Box 608
> Sheridan, WY 82801, USA

Copyright © 1985 by Marilyn F. Grams, MD

First Printing 1985
Second Printing May 1986
Published and printed in the United States of America

Library of Congress Cataloging in Publication Data

Grams, Marilyn , 1950-
> Breastfeeding success for working mothers.

> Bibliography: p.
> Includes index.
1. Breastfeeding
2. Women--Employment.
 I. Title.
RJ216.G68   1985   649'.33   85-71326
ISBN 0-932707-14-9   (pbk.)

Dedication:

To you and your new baby.
May you have as much fun breastfeeding your baby as I had breastfeeding mine.

Acknowledgements

SPECIAL THANKS to my husband, Wendell J. Robison MD, who talked me into having children; to Dorothy Skye MD who helped with the birthing of my children and the start of this book; and to Mindy Bingham and Dan Poynter who showed me how to finish this book.

WHILE IT WOULD BE IMPOSSIBLE to name every person and source whose data and ideas influenced my thoughts, I do want to thank the following people for their inspiration, criticism, key concepts and/or encouragement: Velma Bacak MD, Irene Biffar RN, Mary Chaffee RN, the Reverand Julia Osborne Christensen, Eileen Curran, Alice Gerard, Elisabet Helsing, Spencer Johnson MD, Elizabeth Keck, Sheila Kippley, Sheila Kitzinger, the La Leche League International, Ruth A. Lawrence MD, Dee Locke, Linda McCormack RN, Maggi McCreery MD, Ingrid Mitchell, Cherry Moore, Lois Norman, Eileen O'Regan MD, Karen Putnam MD, Karen Sebastionai, Tine Thevenin, and Edith Tibbetts.

Table of Contents

DISCLAIMER

The author of this book is a doctor, but she is *not your doctor.* Her medical specialty is adult Internal Medicine, and she does not render medical advice concerning children or the reproductive problems of women.

This book is designed to provide information in regard to the subject matter covered. It is sold with the understanding that neither the publisher, nor the distributor nor the author is engaged in rendering medical or other professional services.

While the information in this book is quite general and therefore appropriate for most new mothers and most new babies, *there may be some medical reason why some of it is not appropriate for you.* The reader is cautioned to seek the advice of a physician qualified to render maternal and/or child care in regards to her own particular circumstances and for new developments.

Every effort has been made to make this book as complete and as accurate as possible. However, there *may be mistakes* both typographical and in content. Therefore, this book should be used only as a general guide and not as the ultimate source of information about breastfeeding or child rearing. Furthermore, this book contains information on breastfeeding only up to the printing date.

The purpose of this book is soley to educate and entertain; *it is not intended to replace the advice of your physician.* The author, publisher and distributor shall have neither liability nor responsibility to any person or entity with respect to any loss or damage caused or alleged to be caused directly or indirectly by the information contained in this book.

If you do not wish to be bound by the provisions of this disclaimer, send the book and your sales receipt to Achievement Press, P. O. Box 608 Sheridan, WY 82801 for a full refund of your purchase price.

1

Why a Breastfeeding Book for Working Mothers?

Can working mothers breastfeed? Absolutely. Is it difficult for them to do so? It doesn't have to be, if they know what they are doing and have a plan. *Today, one out of every two new American mothers goes back to work outside the home before her baby is one year of age. Breastfeeding can be easier than bottle feeding for this working mother if she knows the secrets of breastfeeding success.*

There is a breastfeeding revolution going on, and working women want to participate just like everyone else. In 1978, thirty-five percent of all American mothers breastfed their new babies. In 1984, sixty-two percent did, and this number will exceed seventy-five percent in the next few years.

Such enthusiasm for breastfeeding hasn't been seen in this country in the last hundred years. Ten

9

years ago doctors tried to convince mothers that breastfeeding was best for their babies. Mothers don't need to be convinced today. *Women know that breastfeeding is important and good, and want to experience this special relationship first-hand.*

Why the rush away from "scientifically" prepared formula back to breastfeeding? In his book *Megatrends* John Naisbitt gave us some insight as he discussed high-tech and high-touch.

We are balancing the technological marvels in our lives with warm, human high-touch opposites. Along with artificial heart operations and intensive care units, we have the booming hospice movement and birthing centers.

We buy Cuisinarts, but prefer the high touch of chopping vegetables by hand. We are turning away from sterile "scientific" approaches to child-rearing and want something more human.

We are human beings and want to experience human experiences. Nothing is more human and fascinating for men and women alike than watching what happens as a baby grows up breastfed.

In the 1960's women began to say "if we are going to have sex, we want to experience orgasm." Now we are saying "if we are going to have babies, we want to experience breastfeeding." We want to explore all the dimensions of our biological natures.

So we have the breastfeeding revolution. But it is a revolution that is falling flat on its face. In many hospitals, eighty percent of all new mothers start out breastfeeding, but many drop out when their babies are less than a week old. At least half of all new "breastfed" babies are getting formula at two weeks of age. Most have left the breast entirely by three months of age, and a baby breastfed for one year (like the American Academy of Pediatrics recommends) is a distinct rarity.

This alarming drop-out rate is occurring nation-wide. US Surgeon General C. Everett Koop recently said it would be a big improvement if just thirty-five percent of all breastfeeding mothers kept nursing their babies for just six months.

WHAT'S HAPPENING HERE? Why are all these new mothers giving up on breastfeeding so quickly? As I awaited the birth of my first baby, it seemed to me every other expectant mother I knew was planning to breastfeed. But when I got back to work, all the other new babies seemed to be getting formula instead, and their mothers were not very happy about it.

I have never seen a mother jump for joy when her baby goes on the bottle. But many have said they wish their breastfeeding experiences had lasted longer. *If today's new mother wants to breastfeed, but all too often ends up bottle feeding, what is going wrong?*

I think there is an **INFORMATION GAP.** Most of us were bottle-fed, and have never been exposed to breastfeeding role models. Many of the doctors we see do not have direct breastfeeding experience, either. *Much of the breastfeeding advice dispensed today is old-fashioned, impractical, and flat-out wrong, dreamed up by male physicians who obviously never tried out their theories.*

WHEN WOMEN GET THE INFORMATION they need, they invariably succeed at breastfeeding. Julius Sedgewick surveyed all of the 2847 babies born in Minneapolis in 1921, and discovered that ninety-six percent were totally breastfed at three months of age.

I like Minnesotans, but I don't think they can do anything the rest of us can't do if we put our minds to it. Knowledge is the key. You can't expect to drive across country without a road map. And if you get lost time and time again, the road map you have probably isn't very good.

As I puzzled about all the new mothers I knew who had failed at breastfeeding, I decided to figure out what was going wrong. I read everything I could lay my hands on about breastfeeding in the year after my second baby was born.

I went through every breastfeeding book in print. My librarians borrowed books that have been gathering dust for up to thirty years. I read veterinary texts. I tackled the medical literature, which is growing by at least five new breastfeeding articles a month.

Most of this was terribly boring material. I waded through some tomes I'm sure no more than fifty people in the world have ever even looked at. But amongst the bushels of chaff I found kernels of absolute brilliance that made my second experience of breastfeeding superb and much easier than you can imagine.

MY ROAD MAP for breastfeeding success has been evolving ever since. Now, as my "baby" looks toward her third birthday, I present what I think is the information today's working mother needs to be as successful at breastfeeding as the Minnesotans were in 1921.

FIRST, you have to *start out right*. Many early breastfeeding failures occur because mothers don't know how to tell if their babies are taking the breast effectively.

SECOND, you need *time alone together* to learn how to breastfeed, just like newlyweds need a honeymoon. It takes a couple of weeks to learn how to nurse a baby and a couple of months to become expert.

THIRD, to successfully breastfeed, you have to *make enough milk*. The nipple stimulation you get as your baby nurses causes milk to be made, and ninety-six percent of all new mothers will make all the milk their babies need if they get enough nipple stimulation.

FOURTH, you need to *get your rest*. Many new mothers give up breastfeeding because they haven't been shown how they can get the nipple stimulation they need while getting their rest, too.

FIFTH, there's a *"puberty"* to breastfeeding that has *to be gotten through* before the real fun begins. Beginner's troubles like sore nipples are temporary and usually last only a week or so. If a new mother doesn't realize this, she may quit before she gets to the best part of her breastfeeding experience.

SIXTH, all new mothers need to *manage their time* effectively to meet all their responsibilities without losing out on time for themselves. If they give up breastfeeding because they think it takes too much time, they will be rudely surprised to find out bottle-feeding can take up even more time.

SEVENTH, a breastfeeding mother must be able to *adapt to change* because her baby will change his breastfeeding habits as he gets older. More than one baby has suddenly "weaned himself" because his mother could not figure out what to do about his changing behavior or a new tooth.

A breastfeeding road map needs to give all new mothers basic information to get started and the strategies they will need to continue in the face of most common breastfeeding problems. Our high breastfeeding drop-out rate tells us that most new mothers aren't getting this basic information.

Working mothers need advanced breastfeeding information as well. Mothers who want to continue breastfeeding after they go back to work need to use two key strategies stay-at-home mothers do not necessarily need, *reverse cycle feeding* and *Meals in Minutes.*

MEALS IN MINUTES is a quick, easy, reliable method for collecting and freezing breast milk for your baby to drink when you are not there.

REVERSE CYCLE FEEDING keeps your baby fed while you are together so he will not be hungry when you are at work. *Combined with Meals in Minutes, this technique makes breastfeeding easier for the working mother than bottle feeding.*

THE RETURN TO WORK should be planned for so breastfeeding can continue, and a decision must be made about when to go back to work. If you follow the strategies in this book, breastfeeding your baby will have *no impact on your workplace,* and your co-workers will not even know what you are up to if you don't tell them.

It probably doesn't matter whether you go back to work when your baby is six weeks or six months old, but you should *plan to go back to work on a Friday rather* than a Monday, so you will have the weekend to recuperate.

Many of my reviewers say the chapter on **TIME MANAGEMENT** is the most worthwhile chapter in this book. *All of us get exactly the same amount of time in a day, but some people do a lot more with their time than others.*

I share a way of looking at priorities and time use that has enabled me to write this book, keep up a medical practice, play with my kids, pursue my avocations, and still goof off more than most people I know.

I have enjoyed breastfeeding my children so much that my second daughter and I have continued our relationship past her second birthday. After the nutritionally important first year, breastfeeding may continue on a comfort-nursing basis until the child weans herself between two and three years of age.

Every woman has a right to breastfeed for as long as she and her child want to keep it up. It is a tragedy every time a nursing couple gives up early because of lack of knowledge. Women who are successful will often breastfeed longer than they originally thought they wanted to because it is so convenient and so much fun.

BREASTFEEDING SUCCESS *is never having to say "I wish it had lasted longer."* For you, that might be when your baby is three months old, or six months, or two and a half years. With the information in this book, you will be able to set your own goals for breastfeeding and make them a reality. Enjoy my book and enjoy breastfeeding your baby.

2

The Basics

Your breasts are made up of fifteen to twenty clusters of milk glands arranged in a circle like the pieces of a pie. A milk duct drains each group of glands and empties into a *milk sac* located under the dark-skinned *aroela* surrounding your nipple. *Nipples and milk sacs are the important parts of the breasts and are all you really need to remember.*

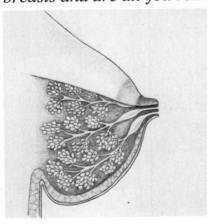

STIMULATING THE NIPPLE will cause milk to be made and released. **SQUEEZING THE MILK SACS** will then empty the breast.

fig. 2-1: THE BREAST. *Remember the nipple and the milk sacs.*

17

NIPPLES AND MILK SACS are the key parts of the breasts. If the nipples are stimulated and the milk sacs are squeezed, everything else will do its job automatically to make milk for your baby.

BREAST SIZE has nothing to do with milk-making ability. All women have about the same number of milk-making glands, so all women are equally capable of making milk for their babies. Women with large busts just have more fatty tissue in their breasts.

NIPPLE STIMULATION causes milk to be made. The more stimulation your nipples get, the more milk will be made. Nipple stimulation also triggers the *let-down reflex*, which must occur if the breasts are to be emptied.

LET-DOWN *is the milk-giving reflex. It must occur for milk to leave the breast. The only reliable way to get let-down started is through direct nipple stimulation,* such as when your baby takes the breast. You may let down in other circumstances and may even let down spontaneously, but if you want to give milk, go where the money is: use direct nipple stimulation.

Unlike the breasts themselves, nipples are rich with nerves, which is why they may be hurt if handled too roughly. Stimulation of these nipple nerves starts the let-down reflex. If a rabbit's nipples are deadened with xylocaine, her babies can nurse but won't get any milk until sensation returns to the nipples and let-down occurs.

From the nipples, the let-down reflex travels through the brain where it can be blocked by worries, fears or distractions. In this way it is similar to a man's sexual functioning. (If a barking dog gets into a dairy barn, the frightened cows quit letting down and the flow of milk ceases. Neither farmer nor milking machine can get a drop of milk until the cows calm down again.)

From the brain, let-down impulses travel to tiny muscles surrounding the milk-making glands in the breasts. These muscles contract, causing milk to flow into the milk sacs, where it pools until these sacs are squeezed.

YOUR BREASTS MAY TINGLE like pins and needles as you let down. (You may not feel this the first few times you nurse your baby, and some women never do.) The breasts tense up and the nipples elongate. Milk streams out of both breasts for a few seconds. For a few days after your baby is born, you may notice mild "after-birth" cramps as you let down. These help your uterus return to its nonpregnant state.

IF YOUR MILK SACS AREN'T SQUEEZED milk flow quickly ceases. But if they are squeezed over and over again, the milk is quickly pumped out of the breast.

Let-down becomes more predictable and certain the more it is used. The more nipple stimulation a nursing mother receives, the more vigorous her let-down will be and the easier it will be to trigger.

HOW YOUR BABY TAKES THE BREAST is critically important to your breastfeeding success. This is called *"latching on."* Many early failures at breastfeeding occur because the baby never learned how to latch on correctly.

IF YOUR BABY TAKES THE BREAST IN THE WRONG WAY, just your nipple will be in his mouth, and you will see most of the dark-skinned areolar tissue outside of his mouth. Your baby will be *frustrated* and *may not nurse effectively,* because he needs stimulation in the back of his mouth for satisfaction and to stimulate his suckling and swallowing reflexes.

You may get *very sore nipples* as your baby gums you in the wrong place, and *swollen painful breasts* because the milk sacs are not being squeezed effectively so the milk is not drained. (This is called *engorgement* and is best prevented by frequent practice nursing sessions.)

IF YOUR BABY TAKES THE BREAST IN THE CORRECT WAY, all of your nipple and much of the surrounding dark-skinned areola will be in his mouth. Your *nipples won't get hurt* because they'll be back away from his gums. Your *breasts will be effectively emptied* because your baby's gums will be compressing the milk sacs.

Your baby will have a full mouthful so he will be *satisfied,* and your nipple in the back of his mouth will stimulate his suck and swallow reflexes, so your baby will *nurse effectively.*

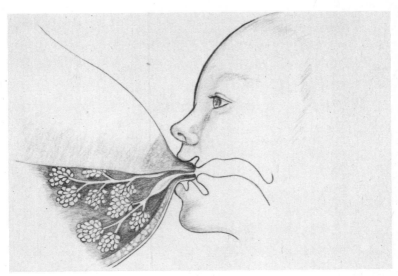

fig. 2-2 (above): THE WRONG WAY to "latch on."

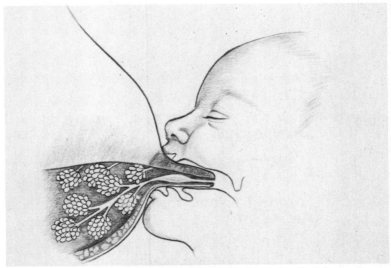

fig. 2-3 (above): THE CORRECT WAY to "latch on."

When your baby latches on correctly, he will immediately start suckling and swallowing, because his suckling and swallowing reflexes are triggered by your nipple in the back of his mouth.

What if he doesn't latch on correctly? If your baby gets just the nipple in his mouth, lift up the corner of his mouth with your finger to break suction. (Just pulling away might hurt your nipple.)

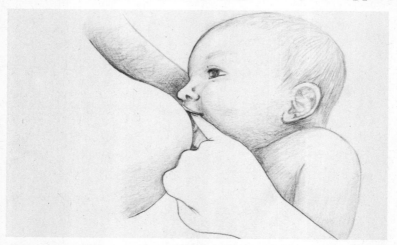

figure 2-4: HOW TO TAKE YOUR BABY OFF THE BREAST *without getting your nipple hurt.*

Then, stroke your baby's cheek with your nipple. This triggers his *rooting reflex.* He will move his head back and forth, searching for the nipple. The more he searches, the wider he opens his mouth. When his mouth opens wide enough, let him take the breast. Keep teasing him in this way until he takes the breast correctly.

After a few little sucks, an effectively nursing baby gets a look of concentration on his face, often with his eyes tightly closed. Then he starts sucking vigorously, moving the little muscles around his ears.

As milk lets down, he may audibly gulp. Then he sucks in spells, nursing and pausing, but staying on the breast. If he mainly wants a meal, he will tank up quickly and leave the breast when he is full.

If he needs some comfort and reassurance, your baby may linger indefinitely until he either falls asleep and his mouth slips off or he is gently taken off the breast.

Nature has no great expectations for the first few nursing sessions. If the baby latches on correctly and gives a few good sucks, he is doing well. Then, over the next few days, he will learn how to nurse and the mother's milk will come in.

BABIES ARE BORN WITH EXTRA FLUID in their tissues and special calorie-rich brown fat to tide them over this learning period. (Brown fat is what makes it possible for bears to hibernate all winter.) Unless your baby is premature or has medical problems, you can rest assured that he is getting enough with your breast milk and does not need supplemental bottles of any kind.

HOSPITAL STAFF MEMBERS are often a bit uncomfortable about breastfeeding because they don't know much about it. There always seems to be at least one caretaker who insists on giving water bottles to breastfed babies. *This is unnecessary, and may confuse some babies who are figuring out how to nurse.*

(When I was a new mother, it seemed to me the main thing the nurses wanted to know was whether my baby had urinated yet or not. In the old days, babies were not given anything by mouth for hours or even a couple of days after birth because doctors mistakenly thought this was best. Now the hospital staff anxiously awaits each baby's first urination. For my babies this happened at the end of the twenty-four hour "normal" range, by which time I was a nervous wreck.)

YOU ARE VERY IMPRESSIONABLE just after your child is born. You will probably find yourself imitating the care nurses give your child. This can threaten your breastfeeding success. If an aid seems nervous and wants to give your baby a bottle, you will have to consciously resist the temptation to do the same.

I diapered, dressed and held my babies just like the nurses did. Because some of the hospital staff worried and gave breastfed babies bottles, I got worried, too.

I succumbed to the worry and tried giving my first baby a bottle of water on her second day of life. She wouldn't take it. I was so inexperienced I still worried after that.

Thoughts of feeding a bottle haunted me like thoughts of smoking had when I was in High School and some college girls tried to get me to smoke. For months I got sudden urges to imitate their smoking behavior, and sometimes had nightmares about it.

It took will power to resist this temptation to conform, but I did because I wanted to be in control of my life.

FORMULA MANUFACTURERS have their feet in the door at too many American hospitals. They hand out free formula samples to bottle-feeding and breastfeeding mothers alike. In the kit given breastfeeding mothers is a booklet of breastfeeding advice with congratulations to the new mother for deciding to breastfeed.

This is advertising, and their breastfeeding advice is suspect. These formula manufacturers don't want you to breastfeed. They want you to buy formula. They want a bottle of formula in your home, hoping you will lose confidence in yourself and reach for it in a weak moment.

If they offer you formula samples, turn them down. If they give them to your husband, throw them out. *Later in your breastfeeding career you may choose to use formula, but while you are learning and impressionable, avoid the wrong crowd and don't keep formula in your house.*

THE FIRST MONTH OR TWO of your baby's life may be worse for you than my internship was for me. During my internship I was on call in the hospital every third night. Up much of the night,

I got phone calls every time I did get to sleep. *But until your baby is a couple of months old, you will probably have to feed him every two or three hours all night long every single night!*

Believe me, you'll need your rest.

If you bottle-fed, someone would have to get up and fix a bottle every time your baby woke up, and before the baby got fed, the whole household would be wide awake. If you breastfeed and sit up in a chair every time you nurse your baby, it still won't be very restful.

MANY NURSING POSITIONS are possible. I like lying down best because you can rest better in this position. Lying-down nursing is an important strategy for several reasons and is discussed more fully in chapters six and seven.

When you lie down to nurse, your baby can be beside you or on top of you. When you sit up to nurse, your baby can be in your lap or under your arm. The latter is sometimes called the "football" position because it is somewhat like holding a football. If your baby is tense and arches her head back a lot, you may find the football position to be the most effective way to nurse her.

IF YOU HAVE TWINS life will be easiest if you learn how to nurse both at once, using pillows to support them so your hands are free.

fig. 2-5 (opposite): **MANY DIFFERENT NURSING POSITIONS ARE POSSIBLE.** Choose some that are comfortable for you.

NOSE BREATHING IS MANDATORY for newborn babies because they haven't yet learned how to breathe through their mouths. If your baby seems to have trouble breathing at the breast, make sure his nose isn't being compressed .

Your baby needs to be close to nurse so that he won't tug on your nipple and make it sore. His nose should touch your breast -- just make sure it's not completely buried.

If your baby has a cold and is stuffed up, use a bulb syringe to clean out his nose before nursing as directed by your doctor.

HOW OFTEN YOUR BABY WILL WANT TO NURSE depends on your baby. There is a broad range of normal feeding patterns for newborns, but most will want to eat every two to three hours around the clock for their first six to eight weeks of life. Then things rapidly get better!

(Just remember bottle-feeding parents get to go through this stage, too. While you are reaching for your baby to nurse, they will be getting up, going to the kitchen, and fixing formula while their babies howl.)

In the beginning, breastfeeding babies tire rapidly and fall asleep quickly. Nipples aren't used to being suckled, and will be sore for the first twenty to thirty times your baby nurses.

Because of these factors you should plan on relatively short, frequent nursing sessions at the start. Just how long they last should be left to your discretion. Have your husband take your watch home and leave it there!

Take your time getting positioned comfortably, and let your baby take his time latching on. If he doesn't seem interested enough to open his mouth wide, stroke his cheek to trigger his rooting reflex. Then he should get down to business.

If your baby often falls asleep before taking the second breast, try burping him or changing his diaper. This stimulation will usually wake him up again enough to get him to nurse at the other side. If this doesn't work, offer the other side first the next time you nurse.

BABIES HAVE UNIQUE PERSONALITIES from birth, and this can be seen in their nursing habits. Some are born hungry and nurse frequently from the start. Others are "lazy" and just not very interested for several days. (Remember they have extra food and water on board, so they don't have to get interested right away.) Some babies tank up quickly and are satisfied, while others seem to savor each mouthful before they swallow it.

You will soon become the world's leading expert on your baby's nursing habits. Whenever it seems appropriate, offer your baby the breast. Let him nurse until he seems satisfied. In a couple of weeks you will be reading each other like a book, and you will feel confident you know how to nurse.

BABIES OFTEN PREFER ONE BREAST to the other. Both of my babies liked the left side best, perhaps because my heartbeat was louder on that side. *If you don't want to become lopsided, make sure your baby nurses at the less favorite breast, too!*

YOU WILL MAKE ENOUGH MILK to meet your baby's needs if you get enough nipple stimulation. For the first month or two, you will probably need to nurse three or more hours per twenty-four hour period. After that, an average of two or more hours should keep your milk supply plentiful.

If your baby has a weak suck it will take more nursing time than otherwise to make enough milk and get your baby fed. (It takes more time than usual to bottle feed a weakly sucking baby, too.)

GROWTH SPURTS occur in all babies, and can scare the socks off new parents the first few times they occur. During growth spurts, babies become ravenously hungry because they are growing faster and need more food.

Growth spurts commonly occur at three to five days, three weeks, six weeks, and three months, but can occur at any time. Your baby's first growth spurt is likely to start just about the time you get home from the hospital, so your first few days at home are an especially stressful time.

USE THE TWENTY-FOUR HOUR peak production plan to handle growth spurt crises. Sheila Kitzinger describes this strategy in her breastfeeding book. Crawl in bed with your baby for twenty-four hours, and let him nurse all he wants to. He will totally drain you dry, but let him keep nursing.

Within twenty-four hours of taking this "horse cure," you'll have much more milk than your baby wants, and the crisis will be over. (Ms. Kitzinger writes that when she had twins, the twenty-four hour peak production plan took only twelve hours, because two babies provided much more nipple stimulation than one, so more milk was made even faster!)

REMEMBER THESE KEY POINTS:

THE KEY PARTS OF THE BREAST are the milk sacs and the nipples. The nipples must be stimulated for let-down to occur, and the milk sacs must be compressed effectively for milk to leave the breast.

THE LET-DOWN REFLEX MUST OCCUR for milk to be released from your breasts. This reflex starts with nipple stimulation, travels through the brain where it can be inhibited, and causes milk to flow from the milk-producing glands to the milk sacs.

WHEN YOUR BABY IS LATCHED ON THE RIGHT WAY, your nipple and dark-skinned areola are in your baby's mouth. The nipple is back behind your baby's gums where it stimulates his suck and swallow reflexes. The milk sacs are in the right position to be compressed as the baby nurses.

IF YOUR BABY LATCHES ON THE WRONG WAY, only your nipple is in his mouth. This leads to an unsatisfied baby, sore nipples, and unemptied breasts. If your baby latches on incorrectly, break suction, and tease his cheek with your nipple until he opens his mouth wide enough to take the breast properly.

NURSING BABIES DON'T NEED BOTTLES. They are born with extra food and water to tide them over the breastfeeding learning period.

YOU ARE IMPRESSIONABLE after your baby is born, and may easily be influenced by what other people say and do. Don't change your mind about breastfeeding during your baby's first two weeks of life. Stick to your original plans. You'll be glad you did.

LYING DOWN IS MY FAVORITE NURSING POSITION, because it is the most restful and gives the baby the most control over his head position, which makes swallowing easier for him.

GROWTH SPURTS RESPOND to marathon nursing sessions. Stay in bed with your baby all day and night, and let him nurse even when you are totally empty. By the next morning the crisis will be over.

A SOLID KNOWLEDGE OF THE BASICS is your first step to breastfeeding success. Keep these key points in mind during your hectic first few weeks of parenthood, and you will soon be a pro at nursing your baby. Now, let's talk about puberty.

3

Puberty, Again?

When your baby is born, your breasts change from being innocent bystanders to the central role in the miracle of lactation. Soon they will be producing all the milk your baby needs to grow and thrive for his first four to six months of life.

This is not an easy job for the breasts, and they have to go through a transition period to gear up for it. I call this transition period the **PUBERTY OF BREASTFEEDING**. The best part about it is that it doesn't last very long. During this period the breasts learn how to make, store, and give milk, and they get used to being suckled.

When these tasks are complete, the puberty of breastfeeding is over. This puberty is nowhere near as long as adolescence. In fact, some parts are over in a few days.

TO MAKE MILK, your breasts have to fully develop. Breast development began before you were born and continued during adolescence. By the time your first baby is born, this development is almost complete. But the finishing touches don't come until your baby starts nursing.

SWELLING AND TENDERNESS result from this preparation of the breasts to make milk. Extra food and energy are brought to the milk-making glands via the blood stream. With this extra blood flow comes extra fullness and fluid in the tissues. Your breasts will become tender and swollen right after your baby is born because of this temporary increase in blood flow.

All new mothers experience the same tenderness and swelling whether they nurse their babies or not. Women who breastfeed actually have an advantage because their babies' nursing empties the milk as it is made, relieving additional pressure.

NURSING BRAS have cups that can be opened up for nursing without taking the bra off. They are a must for nursing mothers, even women who don't normally wear bras, because they will give support to full, achy breasts and they hold nursing pads to absorb the leaks that are common for the first few months.

Because your breasts get larger throughout pregnancy, you shouldn't buy nursing bras before your eighth or ninth months, or they will end up being too small after your baby is born.

Breast swelling and tenderness is a problem for all new mothers for the first three to five days and can be minimized by frequent nursing sessions with your baby. You will have a tendency to be tender when full for a couple of months as your breasts develop storage capacity.

Many women end up wearing maternity tops home from the hospital because they can't get into their regular clothes. Count on having a bigger bust size than usual for the first few months you nurse until your breasts develop storage capacity.

STORAGE CAPACITY has to be developed each time you nurse a new baby. Your breasts will be smaller when your baby is three months old than when he is one month, even though you'll be making much more milk at three months. This is because breast swelling has been replaced by storage capacity.

LEAKAGE will probably occur until your breasts develop storage capacity. If this isn't handled properly, it can be embarrassing enough to make you think about quitting breastfeeding. A doctor friend of mine leaked through her clothes while talking to a patient at the end of a long emergency room shift, and was mortified enough she quit breastfeeding.

GOOD NURSING PADS can prevent this from happening to you. Nursing pads are inserts for your nursing bra that absorb leakage and keep you dry. Good nursing pads will absorb leakage for eight to twelve hours without falling apart or getting your clothes wet.   They are made of cloth or absorbent materials and keep you dry while allowing your skin to "breathe."

(In the old days, women were advised to use rubber devices or Saran Wrap to collect leakage, and sometimes had problems with skin breakdown, nipple soreness, and infection from a "sweat suit" effect. This won't happen with modern nursing pads.)

Most nursing pads are circles of absorbent material three to four inches in diameter. Evenflo, Gerber, Johnson and Johnson and others make inexpensive disposable pads that are convenient to use. Some baby shops will also have washable cloth ones.

Cloth nursing pads may have a role after your storage capacity is developed, where there is just a little leakage to be absorbed. If cloth pads get too wet, they can dry onto your nipples and pull off the top layer of skin when removed!

Not all disposable nursing pads are created equal. I liked Evenflo's best because their outer layer kept my clothes dry even if they were otherwise soaking wet, and they kept me dry for up to twelve hours on the rare occasions where I was unable to nurse or express milk. Some of the other major brand-name nursing pads soaked through in a couple of hours and disintegrated like wet facial tissues.

SORE NIPPLES result from the suction your baby generates as he takes the breast and the action of his tongue as he nurses. Suction is a vacuum effect and is broken as soon as milk flows into your baby's mouth. This is why you may get an "ouch" for the first few seconds as your baby takes the breast.

As you are getting through the "ouch" stage of breastfeeding, take a couple of deep breaths to relax as your baby takes the breast, and offer the least sore side first. You may want to massage your nipples and the surrounding dark-skinned areola to stimulate let-down before your baby nurses to prevent any delays in the flow of milk.

You may develop blisters and even bleed a little during this toughening-up process. This is normal and will quickly resolve because the skin heals so rapidly. Let a little breast milk dry on your sore nipples. This is better than ointments and cremes for lubricating and preventing infections, and it doesn't cause skin rashes. Breast milk also tastes better.

Your nipples will toughen up rapidly. After the first twenty to thirty nursing sessions, the worst is past. Nurse frequently despite a little discomfort for the first two or three days, and you'll be just about over the sore nipple stage by the time you go home from the hospital. *The quicker you learn to let down even though it hurts a little, the faster you will be past the sore nipple stage.*

PRENATAL NIPPLE PREPARATION is sometimes advised as a way of preventing sore nipples. I don't think it provides any benefits for most women. Rubbing the nipples vigorously with a towel cannot simulate your baby's suction and tongue action, and it is this suction and tongue action that causes blisters and soreness.

If your husband suckles at your breasts, he might toughen them up a little, but don't get carried away with this because nipple stimulation has been used as a method of inducing labor!

It is said that eighteenth century wet nurses got sore nipples each time they took on a new baby to nurse, presumably because each baby's mouth and suckling patterns are different, so the suckling and tongue action are applied differently.

The only time I might recommend prenatal nipple preparation is if you have an *inverted nipple* or nipples. In this situation, the nipple is tucked back into the breast so it doesn't even get rubbed by your clothing. It can be quite a shock for such a protected nipple to experience the suckling action of a hungry newborn.

One La Leche League mother reported her experiences with one normal nipple and one inverted nipple. With her first three babies, she did no prenatal nipple preparation, and the inverted nipple was much sorer than the other one.

Before her forth baby was born, she drew the inverted nipple out a few times a day by squeezing gently on the line where the dark skin of the aroela meets the regular skin color of the breast. As she did this, the hidden nipple appeared. (She could also have used gentle suction to draw the nipple out.)

Then she pulled the inverted nipple out as far as it would come and rubbed and rolled it around for a few minutes. With this preparation, her inverted nipple was much less sore than it had been the other times she nursed.

SPONTANEOUS LET-DOWN is an amusing part of breastfeeding puberty. This is where you suddenly let down in circumstances unrelated to your baby. It's like having a built-in fun meter because spontaneous let-down doesn't occur if you are not enjoying yourself.

If you're happy, pleased with yourself, or anticipating good things, you may tingle, tense up and feel the flow of milk. This often happened to me as I got to my babysitter's house. With good nursing pads, no one in the world has to know why you just got a little smile on your face.

You can press back on your nipples with the heels of your hands to stop the flow of milk, but it quickly stops on its own anyway because the milk sacs are not being compressed.

As you repeatedly experience let-down in the settings where you want to give milk, your reflex will mature and spontaneous let-down will become unusual.

BREASTFEEDING PUBERTY is the transition period where your breasts learn how to make milk, store milk, give milk, and be suckled. It is much shorter than adolescence. Tender breasts and sore nipples last just a few days, and the leaking lessens rapidly after the first couple of months.

Understanding how your body works makes the uncomfortable aspects of these changes a brief stop on your road to breastfeeding enjoyment and success.

4

The Babymoon

Did you take your mother along on your honeymoon? Of course not. Society recognizes the need for newlyweds to be away by themselves in a private setting. Marriage is a major transition, and the new couple needs time alone by themselves to get to know each other and to adjust.

But marriage isn't the most extreme transition in your life. The birth of a child is. With marriage you start out with someone you know, love, and have chosen, and it's still a big step.

With a new baby, you are attached for life to a total stranger, who is helpless to boot! You have an even bigger transition to make than with a new mate. For this transition to be successful, you need a babymoon. Sheila Kitzinger talked about it in her book, *The Experience of Breastfeeding.*

41

THE BABYMOON takes place primarily in the bedroom, with brief forays to the outside world for food and drink. It's like a honeymoon, and like a honeymoon it's a private affair. It gives the new family a chance to come to grips with the tremendous change in their lives.

Although the father and older children have to get to know their new baby too, the central figures in the babymoon are the nursing mother and her baby, because they have to function effectively on a biological level if breastfeeding is to be successful.

Allow two weeks for the babymoon, because it takes a couple of weeks to learn how to nurse. You won't be flying off together to the Bahamas, but you need to have the same sense of privacy and freedom from responsibilities that you would if you did physically get away from all the friends, relatives and neighbors who want to see your new baby and offer advice.

You are in a very impressionable state of mind when you come home from the hospital, so it's best for your breastfeeding success if you are cloistered away from outside influences until you and your baby figure out what you are doing.

In many societies, new mothers and their babies are kept alone together for the first couple of weeks and have very little contact with other people except when food and drink are brought to them. They most definitely do not cook, wash clothes, clean house or entertain at this time!

A little foresight will enable you to enjoy your babymoon even if you aren't waited on hand and foot. Fast foods and frozen dinners were designed for times like this. Since you don't want the neighbors to come over in droves anyway, let the house stay messy so you'll be too embarrassed to let them in.

If your husband hasn't been trained to do the laundry, now's the time for him to learn. Most men, given the choice between diapering a new baby and doing housework will choose housework every time, so it's not hard to clarify whose job supper and the dirty clothes are.

IT SHOULD BE EASY for a working mother on maternity leave to get several hours a day alone with her baby, while daddy and the older children do what they usually do during the day.

There is no reason to change everyone's routine just because there is a new addition to the family, and there are good reasons not to. Father and the older kids won't vie for your attention if they are away at work, school or the babysitter's.

They will probably find the transition in their lives easier if they have the continuity of their usual activities during the day, and this leaves you and your new baby alone for your babymoon.

STAY IN BED all day if you want to. There's plenty of room in the middle of a double bed to nurse with abandon without your baby falling off the edge of the bed. When you are ready to take a nap, move over a little so you won't have to worry about smothering your baby. Make sure he can't fall off the bed. Then, snuggle up close and enjoy your new baby.

YOU'RE ABOUT TO HAVE a peak experience unlike anything other than falling in love. Sooner or later in this setting of privacy, closeness and physical contact, this will no longer be a baby, but will become your baby.

From that moment on you won't be able to remember what life was like without this person in it. You are bonded now and deserve a babymoon to savor the richness of this experience.

With this outpouring of emotion comes the outpouring of milk. It is virtually impossible not to let down freely in this setting. And think how fortunate you are as a nursing mother that you don't have to interrupt your reverie to open a can of formula.

As you practice you'll get better and better at breastfeeding. Every successfull encounter teaches you and your baby how to be more successful the next time around. Practice makes perfect, and the babymoon is the ideal place to practice until you both know what you are doing and are ready to face the rest of the world.

SURVIVAL for new parents requires keeping things simple. Have your husband buy disposable diapers, and keep plenty on hand. My new babies went through ten to twelve a day. Have enough baby clothes on hand so you don't run out too often. Your baby may throw up if he is trying to nurse with his head turned to the side because it is harder to swallow in that position. You'll probably have to change clothes every time this happens.

Breastfed babies have soft stools that can be pretty runny, especially the first week or so as your early milk (called colostrum) exerts its beneficial laxative effect. Even with fitted disposable diapers, in the first couple of months I never managed to get through a day without having to change my baby's clothes at least once for this reason.

Don't get up in a chair to nurse during your babymoon except on rare occasions. It's easier for your baby to find a good head position and swallow easily if you both lie down on your sides facing one another. And it's much more restful.

I THINK YOU SHOULD EAT ONLY "favorite foods" during your babymoon. My definition of favorite foods is anything that tastes good and can be fixed, heated up, or picked up on the way home from work in half an hour or less.

If there is any time in your life when you need comforting, familiar foods, it is during your babymoon. Whatever you ate during pregnancy produced a good baby, so there is no reason to change your diet now just because you are nursing your baby.

HELP from a grandparent or other relative can be invaluable to a busy new family, but think a bit about the best timing. It won't necessarily be as soon as the baby is born. In fact, because you are insecure and vulnerable at this time, the presence of a Grandmother may be too intimidating, especially if this is your first baby.

If a relative wants to come to help out, consider asking for help for the time you are going back to work. My mother stayed for about a month after I went back to work, and it was much more helpful than it would have been right after my baby was born.

THE KEYS TO A SUCCESSFUL BABYMOON are privacy, practice, and freedom from everyday responsibilities. You and your baby enter your babymoon as strangers and emerge as a nursing couple, ready for the challenges and enjoyment of a successful breastfeeding experience.

5

Comfort Nursing

"Breastfeeding" isn't a very good name for what goes on between a mother and her nursing infant. There's much more to this experience than just getting calories into Junior. Not all researchers realize this, and some try to measure breastfeeding as if it were the generic equivalent of bottle feeding.

THE FIVE-MINUTE QUICKIE SYNDROME is an unfortunate result of some inaccurate breastfeeding research which supposedly showed that babies can empty the breast in five minutes. Mothers are sometimes led to believe they should not let their babies nurse longer than that.

Nothing could be more disasterous than that impression. Mothers who routinely take their babies off the breast after five minutes are destined to have problems and will probably lose their milk when the going gets rough.

Why?

First of all, this research is not accurate. *How long it takes to empty the breast depends on how experienced and hungry your baby is, how full you are, and how easily you let down. These factors vary from feeding to feeding.*

When a three-month old is seriously hungry he probably can tank up and drain you dry in ten minutes. But while he is learning it takes longer. Sometimes he just wants to play, and your let-down isn't like a switch that can be turned on and off at will.

Sometimes it takes longer to let down than others. When you're winding down from a hectic day it might take you longer than five minutes just to let down. And as you know, the milk doesn't flow until let-down occurs.

Besides being inaccurate, this five-minute quickie mentality is misleading. Dangerously so. If you limit the amount of time your baby is at the breast, you won't have enough milk, and your baby won't be very satisfied. It takes nipple stimulation to make milk. The more stimulation, the more milk is made.

The strongest urge your baby is born with is the urge to suckle. Mother nature designed it that way to make sure your baby will have enough milk. If you satisfy your baby's suckling urges at the breast, you will have no problem with your milk supply. *If you use pacifiers, you are diverting valuable suckling stimulation and may have trouble making enough milk.*

Babies are pretty flexible. If they get their quota of suckling and cuddling sometime during the day or night they don't care too much exactly when they get it.

So give your baby long leisurely nursing sessions at your convenience and he will be satisfied with "quickies" when you are in a hurry. Work together as a team and everyone benefits.

Comfort is the major benefit your baby gets at the breast, not nutrition. There is nothing in the world as comforting to a crying infant than being picked up and offered the breast.

COMFORT NURSING is offering the breast when your baby is upset, even if he isn't hungry. It is absolutely the best thing you can do, and what you instinctively want to do, so it is very satisfying for both you and your baby.

I've heard at least fifty different suggestions on what to do when your baby is crying, everything from walking the floors to giving the baby a bath to taking a ride in the car to closing the bathroom door on the screaming kid.

But nothing works nearly as well as taking your baby to the breast and letting him drown his sorrows. *The breast is the ultimate pacifier, and should be offered freely.*

When in doubt offer the breast, if you are in situation where you feel comfortable doing so. If not, make up for it later with an "I could tell you were upset" session.

If your baby has learned to seek comfort at the breast, you will sail through crises that end many other women's nursing careers.

I WAS UNDER THE INFLUENCE of the five-minute quickie mentality with my first baby. I viewed breastfeeding as feeding only and was not aware of the concept of comfort nursing.

Sarah sought the breast when she was hungry, and was used to getting a quick meal. We had been nursing for months, and I almost always let down readily.

Then one day she sprouted a tooth and bit me. I yelped and pulled away. She cried as if her heart was broken. I got her calmed down and she took the breast again, but I couldn't let down. I was afraid she was going to bite me again.

We worked things out, but it was shaky. If I couldn't let down quickly, Sarah lost interest quickly. It only took two or three more times to teach her not to bite, but two weeks later she was not nursing any more.

She had decided she could get an easier meal elsewhere.

Although I had enjoyed breastfeeding Sarah for over ten months before that first tooth came in, I was disappointed. I had wanted to breastfeed for a year and had fallen short of my goal. I didn't feel successful because I wished it had lasted longer.

With my second baby it did.

Susan got her first tooth at four months. But she loved to nurse and loved the breast so much that we did not have a crisis. By then I knew about comfort nursing and had always offered her the breast freely.

She had drowned her sorrows at the breast so many times before that when Susan got scolded for nipping me, she turned right back to the breast for comfort. She didn't mind that I couldn't let down right away because for her there had always been more to this relationship than just a meal.

It was comfort she sought right then anyway, not food. After two or three more episodes, Susan had also learned never to bite at the breast. What had ended Sarah's nursing career didn't even put a strain on Susan's because of the value of comfort nursing.

NURSING STRIKES are where, for some reason, a baby suddenly refuses to take the breast. This might occur during teething when the baby's gums are sore, or at the six-month "separation anxiety" stage, where your baby will scream if you leave the room. If he gets mad enough at you, he may give you the cold shoulder and pull away.

Many breastfeeding relationships have ended over some little misunderstanding that resulted in a nursing strike, especially if the mother didn't know what to do next. Nursing strikes usually occur where pacifiers are used and the babies are fed quickly. Since you enjoy and know the value of comfort nursing, you're not likely to get into this situation.

(If your baby does go on strike, wait until he is sleepy or asleep and take him to the breast. He'll nurse like his old self and probably won't be mad at you any more when he wakes up!)

COMFORT NURSING is part of the quality of breastfeeding that makes it a unique and delightful experience. It's what mothers instinctively want to do, so go ahead. Follow your heart. It's the right thing to do.

Comfort nursing strengthens your bond and makes you unique in your baby's eyes, for no one else loves him in this way. It helps you make milk, and assures you that when the going gets rough your baby won't abandon you for a bottle.

Comfort nursing is a key strategy for breastfeeding success.

6

Lying-Down Nursing

Lying down is the best nursing position for you because it is the most restful. Because it is so restful you will find yourself allowing your baby to nurse longer than you would while sitting up. The longer your baby nurses, the more milk you will make and the more satisfied and plump your baby will be.

ALL NEW MOTHERS NEED THEIR REST, especially during the first six to eight weeks when their babies are waking up to eat so frequently. Rest is also of critical importance to working mothers as they return to work and find themselves pressed for time.

Your challenge will be in finding the time to get both your rest and the nursing time needed to make milk and satisfy your baby. *You will need at least two hours of nipple stimulation per twenty-four hour period to maintain a steady milk supply, and three or more hours to increase it.*

THE ONLY PRACTICAL WAY you can get this necessary nipple stimulation and your rest is to combine the two events. This means nursing while lying down because lying down is most restful.

A GOOD TIME for a lying-down nursing session is when you get home from work. It feels so good to get your feet up and relax! You will be achy full and appreciative of your baby's efforts.

You won't feel like cutting this nursing session short, so your baby will get to nurse to his heart's content. It is much more fun to nap with your baby in the afternoon than to wash bottles and prepare formula!

Ask your babysitter to stall a little if your baby seems hungry shortly before you are due to arrive. That way he will be eager to nurse, and soon he will be looking forward to this get-together as much as you do.

Nursing is the easiest way to get your baby to sleep for the night, and nursing in bed is a more pleasant way to wake up in the morning than a frantic race for a bottle would be!

A GOOD PLACE for your lying-down nursing sessions might be a double bed. If your baby is in the middle there should be plenty of room for you to stretch out on one side, and enough space on the other side so that he won't fall off the bed.

WHEN YOUR BABY LEARNS to roll over, or if he is very active and wiggly, push your bed up against the wall, and keep your baby between you and the wall.

Or move to the floor. We put a double-sized mattress on the floor with teddy-bear sheets, and our kids would still rather sleep on that than in their own beds.

LIE ON YOUR SIDES facing one another, and snuggle up close. Your baby will be able to move his head around enough to find his best position for nursing, so he will be less likely to choke as he swallows than in other positions .

Sooner or later you will probably doze off lying down and wake up an hour or more later, rested, with your baby still sleepily suckling at the breast. (Babies have been known to stay at the breast and suckle off and on in their sleep for hours.)

Guess what? With absolutely no effort you will have just gotten half of the minimum daily suckling time you need to maintain your milk supply, while getting your rest, too.

As long as you are comfortable, it is fine for your baby to indulge in sleepy suckling. If he gets to do this some of the time, at your convenience, he will be satisfied with a five-minute quickie when you are in a hurry.

Breastfeeding is something you and your baby can do in your sleep!

BREASTFEEDING CAN BE POSSIBLE even in unusual work situations if you use lying-down nursing. I was able to keep nursing my first baby even though I was away from home every other night, thanks to this technique.

When Sarah was five months old, I spent five weeks in the Intensive Care Unit as an Internal Medicine resident. It was like having forty-eight hour days, for we were often up all night every other night, and would go home to catch up on sleep every other afternoon.

I collected milk at work three or four times during each shift at the hospital, and picked Sarah up on my way home. When my husband came home every other evening he found us in the middle of the bed asleep and nursing away.

I did not really know what I was doing at the time, but it is fortunate we happened to take those long nursing naps together, for without the nipple stimulation these naps gave me, our breastfeeding relationship would have ended that month.

CHOKING PROBLEMS in young breastfed infants can often be solved by lying-down nursing. I figured this out with my second baby, but did not know why it worked until later.

Susan nursed lustily from the start. My milk came in quicker than with my first baby, and my let-down was vigorous. I had nursed my first baby in a rocking chair, but I quickly learned Susan could not handle this position.

Every time I tried to nurse her sitting up, Susan choked and threw up. I tried stimulating let-down first and having her take the breast after the flow had slackened, but this did not help. I got pretty tired of changing clothes all the time.

I soon noticed Susan did not throw up when we nursed lying down, so that became our preferred position. After she was two months old, we were able to learn how to nurse sitting up, but still preferred to lie down because it was so much more restful and fun.

Why would lying down be such a good position for a baby to swallow in? Because it is the easiest way for a young infant to keep his head in a neutral straight-ahead position, and swallowing with your head in any other position can be difficult.

It is hard to swallow with your head tilted back, or your chin tucked down, or your chin touching your shoulder. (Try it!) It is also hard to hold a baby in your arms in a way so that he can take the breast without tilting his head too much. And if his head is tilted too much, he won't be able to swallow very well and may choke.

Babies do not gain the strength to hold up their heads for several months. But from birth they can turn their heads from side to side to seek the breast as long as they do not have to work against the forces of gravity.

Lie on your side and bring your baby towards your breast as he lies on his side. He will be looking straight ahead with his head in a good swallowing position. Then he can latch in his most comfortable swallowing position, and all you have to do is relax.

If your baby chokes as you breastfeed in other positions, try nursing lying down. It allows your baby the most control over his head position, and therefore allows him to swallow most comfortably and effectively. I think you will be as pleased as I was with the difference this can make.

THERE ARE THREE BASIC POSITIONS for your lying-down nursing sessions.

fig. 6-1: THE STANDARD LYING-DOWN POSITION
has the baby nursing at the lower breast.

IN THE STANDARD POSITION you and your baby face one another while lying on your sides. Your baby latches on to the *lower* breast. When you want to change breasts, move your baby to the other side and roll over. Then he will nurse at the other breast, which is now the lower one.

THE ALTERNATE POSITION has you rolled over onto your stomach a little so your baby can nurse from the *top* breast. *By using both positions you can switch breasts without having to switch sides and move your baby.* The alternate position is a little harder to learn than the standard one, and it may be uncomfortable as long as your breasts are larger than usual and somewhat tender.

fig.6-2: THE ALTERNATE LYING-DOWN POSITION has the baby nursing at the upper breast.

THE THIRD LYING-DOWN NURSING option is where you lie on your back while your baby lies on top. If you have twins, this could be your most valuable reclining position because both babies can nurse at once. See page 27 for an illustration of this and other nursing positions.

IF YOU'RE NOT COMFORTABLE nursing lying down, you may be trying too hard. People sleep lying down because it is so comfortable, but if you twist yourself in unusual ways to connect your baby with the breast you may strain your back.

I had that problem for awhile. I found myself trying to bring my breast to the baby instead of bringing my baby to the breast. This was anything but relaxing. When I realized she could easily latch on if I just brought her close, I relaxed and had no more trouble.

When you nurse lying down get comfortable as if you were going sleep. You can learn to nurse in any position you like to sleep in except flat on your stomach. When you are comfortable bring your baby close and let *him* finish the connection.

Whenever you can, nurse lying down. It is the most restful position for you and the easiest way for your baby to swallow without choking. You will make plenty of milk while getting your rest, and your baby will get the suckling time he loves.

NURSING LYING DOWN is a key strategy for breastfeeding enjoyment and success.

7

Sleeping Arrangements

Where should your baby sleep at night? Off in a room by himself or near you? From a practical standpoint, sleeping next to you is the easiest. In my opinion it is also the safest place for your baby to sleep.

THE FIRST PART of getting a good night's sleep with a new baby is sleeping near your baby. We didn't know that with our first child. We converted our study into a nursery with an expensive crib and a "comfortable" rocking chair.

We were going to be equal-opportunity parents. We had agreed that Wendell would fetch if I would feed in the middle of the night.

I had never taken care of babies before, so I did exactly what the nurses in the hospital told me to do. When they said "never feed your baby until you have changed her diaper first," I thought her bottom would probably rot off if I disobeyed.

When Sarah cried at night, I kicked Wendell out of bed with strict instructions to change her diaper before bringing her to me. If she wasn't mad enough before the lights went on, she certainly was after the diaper had been changed.

Then, after she tanked up, she was wide awake and wouldn't go back to sleep. She certainly didn't want to be ditched all alone in a room by herself, so one of us would lie on the floor by her crib and attempt to sneak out of the room when we thought she had fallen asleep.

We suffered.

Wendell tried bedding Sarah down in a bassinet by the side of the bed so he would wake up before I got mad and kicked him out of bed. But I vetoed the idea. Somehow I thought her little noises would disturb my sleep.

And I didn't think it was OK. I didn't know at the time that more and more American couples are keeping their babies close by at night. I didn't know that the La Leche League endorses this practice, or that Tine Thevenin had written an entire book on the subject.

I wasn't aware that in most other cultures in the world, babies sleep near their mothers for their first year of life, or that this had been the practice in America in the Revolutionary era.

So we suffered.

It took just one night at home with our second child to figure out *the only thing worse than one screaming child in the middle of the night is two screaming children in the middle of the night.*

The first night Susan woke Sarah up screaming, and I moved her bassinet to our room. My only objective was to get to the baby before she woke her sister up.

And guess what?

Not only did I find myself getting to the baby before she woke her sister up, I found myself getting to the baby before she woke herself up!

This blessed child never had to endure an empty stomach, the bright lights, and being alone in the nursery at night like her sister had to do.

And we didn't have to, either.

I got so attuned to Susan's breathing patterns that I woke up if she started to stir. As I looked down I would see slight movements, such as turns of her head in search of the breast, or a little shrug of her shoulder.

Then I would bring her to bed with me to nurse. She would nurse vigorously for ten minutes or so, and then sleepily suckle until I put her back in her bassinet again.

After we trained Susan to sleep at night, she never awoke again at night. Neither did her sister nor her father. Wendell's lack of night-time participation didn't bother me this time around, because I was falling right back to sleep myself.

We all felt much more rested in the mornings with this sleeping arrangement, and the people at work couldn't figure out why we didn't look as exhausted as they thought new parents should.

THE SECOND PART to getting a good night's sleep with a new baby at home is getting your little one to think it's night time when you do.

Both of our babies were born wanting to stay up at night. There's a good chance your baby will want to be awake at night, too, because before they are born, infants have no outside clues as to what time of day it is.

All human beings have biological time clocks that regulate our sleep-wake cycles. Most of us are not ideally suited for life on Earth, because our biological time clocks are not set for twenty-four hour days.

Most of us have biological time clocks set for a few hours longer than twenty-four, which is why most of us find it easy to stay up late at night and hard to get up in the morning. If we get way off our usual sleep-wake cycles, we will be sound asleep sometime during the day and unable to get to sleep at night.

Since most people find it easier to stay up late than get to sleep early, you are likely to have more success keeping your baby awake when he is sleepy than getting him to go to sleep when he's not.

This strategy can be used to change your baby's sleep-wake cycle to coincide with yours, and when this finally occurs, you'll all really be "sleeping through the night."

TO READJUST YOUR BABY'S biological time clock, first figure out when he is sleeping the longest at one stretch. This is his period of deepest sleep and what you want to get cycled around to be the same as yours. Once you have figured out when this time is, you are ready to begin.

Let your baby sleep when he wants to, eat when he wants to, and play when he wants to. Except one time a day. Two hours into that deepest sleep period, wake him up. It may take a bath with loud music playing, or a marathon tickle session, but get him awake. Have him nurse and then let him fall asleep.

By doing this, you have just put your baby on a twenty-six hour day. Keep waking him up once a day, and keep him on a twenty-six hour day until he is dead tired and falls asleep at your bedtime. Then leave him alone.

It took us a couple of weeks to get Susan's biological clock cycled around to coincide with ours. As a newborn, she woke up to nurse every one and a half to two hours, day and night, except that she slept four hours straight between one in the afternoon and suppertime.

The first day she was home Susan ate at one PM and was still asleep at three. I pounced. With great effort I got her awake for a song and a diaper change. Then she nursed and slept until seven.

The next day we woke her at five PM and she slept until nine. Then, awakened at seven, she slept until eleven. In two more days we had her sleeping most soundly when we wanted to be asleep. Then we left her alone.

She got off-cycle a few times but it was easy to get her straightened out again. By the time she was two months old her sleep-wake pattern was so deeply rooted I think we could have thrown her across the room at night without waking her up. She certainly didn't wake up being brought to the breast or put back into her bed after a meal.

WHAT ABOUT THE DIAPERS at night? There is little reason to change a newborn's diaper before a feeding, because he is most likely to have a bowel movement during or after a feeding.

After a couple of months, stooling at night usually becomes infrequent, even though your baby may continue to eat frequently at night. If your baby has a bowel movement after a feeding, change his diaper. If he doesn't, don't bother.

ANOTHER CHOICE for a good night's sleep is to nurse your baby on a bed or mattress in the baby's room. It's private and restful, and not all husbands want to have the baby in their room.

THE SAFETY of sleeping arrangements has been a controversial subject. There are two schools of thought in this area. One school, to which I belong, maintains that it is potentially dangerous for infants less than one year of age to sleep alone.

Human babies are born with very immature nervous systems. While newborn calves get up and take a few steps right after birth, it takes most human babies a year to learn how to walk.

Breathing patterns may be irregular in infants, and there is some concern that SIDS or Sudden Infant Death Syndrome is seen more frequently in babies who have had pauses in their breathing.

Pauses in breathing are most likely to occur if a baby is totally isolated with no human sounds around. Generally if a baby quits breathing, he starts right up again as soon as he is touched, picked up or spoken to.

When we look at the animal kingdom and most other cultures in the world we see mothers staying with their babies at night. It seems prudent to me to follow this time-proven strategy.

THE OTHER SCHOOL OF THOUGHT about sleeping safety holds that it might be potentially dangerous for babies to sleep with their mothers for fear that the mothers could "overlay" or smother their infants.

This concern dates back to the 1800's when the upper classes in Europe hired wet nurses to nurse their children, and actually paid their wages partly in beer and ale.

The newspapers of the day decried the scandal of drunk wet nurses smothering their charges. While this could theoretically happen, it's not at all likely, as long as you're careful.

FOR NURSING SAFETY, REMEMBER THESE GUIDELINES:

DON'T LIE DOWN TO NURSE *your baby if you have been drinking or if you are taking medications that might make you unusually sleepy.*

IF YOU TAKE YOUR BABY TO BED WITH YOU, *make sure he can't fall out of bed, and keep pillows and bed clothes away from his face.*

If you are careful, nursing lying down is easy and restful, and safer, in my opinion, than having your baby off in a room by himself.

Although I could take afternoon naps with my baby at the breast, I slept better at night with her in her bassinet. I placed it on the floor by my side of the bed, up by the headboard so I wouldn't step on her if I got up before I remembered she was there. That way I was able to flail around in my sleep with abandon without hurting my little one.

Many couples I know kept their babies in bed between them most of the time, and would transfer the little ones to their bassinets when they wanted to be alone together.

TRY KEEPING YOUR BABY NEAR YOU at night for his first year of life. It's fun and so easy. I think you will find it as valuable for your breast-feeding success as I found it for mine.

8

Staging Your Comeback: The Return to Work

You have mastered the basics of breastfeeding, and are going through puberty again. You and your baby learned how to nurse on your babymoon and now are becoming experts.

You comfort nurse, and appreciate the value of long leisurely lying-down nursing sessions. You have cycled your baby's biological time clock around so that he thinks it's time for bed when you do.

Now you are probably starting to think about going back to work again. *In order to be a good parent you have to be able to continue your adult life with children.*

I enjoyed my maternity leave but by the time Sarah was five weeks old I noticed I wasn't talking to her much any more. I changed her diapers and fed her but this was not all the excitement and human contact I yearned for.

I was ready to go back to work.

PREPARATION is the key to staging a successful return to work. This will be a major stress point in your nursing relationship and those mothers who are not prepared will probably fail to reach their breastfeeding goals.

FIRST, you need to *collect breast milk* and build up a freezer *breast-milk bank*. We will talk about this in Chapter Nine, "Meals in Minutes."

SECOND, you need to learn how to *keep your baby from being very hungry* while you are away by feeding him frequently when you are together. This is is called reverse cycle feeding. It is the best-kept secret of working mothers and will be discussed in Chapter Ten.

THIRD, you have to think about how you will handle all your responsibilities and still get time for yourself. We will talk about *establishing priorities* and *time management* in Chapter Eleven, "Where Do I Get Enough Time?"

FOURTH, you need to *expand your nursing comfort zone* so you can relax and let down in a variety of settings. After your babymoon there is no reason to be "tied down" to breastfeed.

FINALLY, you have got to *decide when* and how *to go back to work,* arrange child care, and do some practice runs so you will be ready for your first day back on the job.

LET'S TALK ABOUT COMFORT ZONES. My friend Joe is a nationally known speaker who gives seminars for a living. He tells what happened when he got sick and had to convalesce at home for a month.

"My comfort zone shrank to the size of my house. By the end of a month I got nervous just walking out the front door.

"The first time I gave a seminar after I got well my knees knocked all the way to the podium. That was a terrible day. I was scared to death. But I didn't give up. I stayed with it and within a few weeks my comfort zone had stretched right back to where it had been before my illness."

Comfort zones are where we are relaxed and comfortable. They are different for each one of us and different at different times in our lives. They change as our circumstances do.

Your first day back to work will probably be just as bad as Joe's was. Your comfort zone will probably also have become smaller.

Later in this chapter we will discuss how to time your return to work to minimize comfort zone problems in the workplace. But now let's talk about expanding the horizons of your nursing experience.

Comfort zones are like concentric circles. There is a little one in the middle with bigger and bigger ones as you move away from the center. The center will always be where you are the most comfortable and relaxed and is the place for you to retreat to when the going gets rough. For nursing this center is the babymoon situation: private, dark, quiet and secure.

Every time you step out of your comfort zone you get a little anxious. There is stress because you are involved in something new and you are not yet comfortable. If you can stick with it you will get used to the new situation. Then your comfort zone will enlarge.

But if you find yourself in a situation that is too uncomfortable you may get so anxious that you can't cope at all. A child laughed at for forgetting a poem in school may be terrified to speak before a group for the rest of his life.

Yet we cannot grow without stepping outside our comfort zones. The only way to achieve our goals in life is to go after them and this involves doing things we haven't done before.

Your baby's growth and development requires continual stretching of his comfort zone. He starts out comfortable and secure at the breast and rolls over, crawls, stands and walks his way out into the world in his first year of life.

When he steps too far outside his comfort zone he will come back for reassurance. Then he is ready to try again. You have a similar task before you. With the monumental change of parenthood in your life your comfort zone has shrunk. Now you will have to stretch it back.

As you plan your return to work you will need to gradually stretch your comfort zone back out to where it was before you had your baby. You will also need to learn how to be comfortable nursing your baby in a variety of situations.

If you take many tiny steps and get comfortable after each one you can expand your comfort zone to any size you desire. But if you wait and have to take one gigantic step you will be as terrified as the kid in front of class who suddenly forgot what he was supposed to say.

After your babymoon period, when you are confident you know how to nurse, begin to expand your nursing comfort zone. Get out of the bedroom and nurse in other places around the house.

See if you can nurse while doing desk work or using the telephone. *The trick to doing other things while nursing your baby is to not get so distracted that your let-down stops.*

Nurse at home with other people around. You will be comfortable doing this with some people but not others. If it doesn't work out, retire to the privacy of your bedroom.

It is easy to get comfortable nursing your baby outside the home because it's easy to find private places to go where no one will see you. I've nursed my babies in department store changing rooms, rest rooms, and safety deposit box cubicles.

Many tops can be pulled up or unbuttoned discreetly to allow nursing. Pretty soon you will realize other people are busy with their own lives and are paying no attention to what you are doing.

The more experience you get at going out with your baby and nursing in a variety of situations the easier your return to work will be.

WHEN TO GO BACK TO WORK will depend on you and your circumstances. When you start to miss work it is probably time to go back.

Four weeks minimum should be allowed at home with your new baby before you go back to work and six weeks if this is your first baby or your first breastfeeding situation.

A gradual return to work will ensure a smooth transition for you with the least amount of stress. *If you go too fast and get overwhelmed, your milk supply and let down ability will suffer.*

Go back to work on a Friday so you will have the whole weekend to recover. Either work half-days for the first couple of weeks or schedule yourself light and do not do more than you have scheduled.

ALTHOUGH PREGNANCY is not an illness, I like to explain maternity leave to bosses using illness as an analogy. Bosses understand that it takes four to six weeks to get over a heart attack or major surgery. They realize that if an employee overdoes it as he comes back to work he may get sick again. Then he will miss even more work.

Working women have far fewer sick days as a group than working men, including all their time away from work because of pregnancy and childbirth. Don't think you are being unfair to anyone by taking time from work for yourself and your baby because you are not. When a co-worker of yours has a car wreck or gets appendicitis no one begrudges him his time away from work, so no one should begrudge you yours.

Things happened right with my first comeback to work, although I was not smart enough to plan it that way. I got one month maternity leave. A nurse suggested I ask for an additional two weeks regular vacation, and because I was enjoying my freedom from the alarm clock so much I did.

My boss insisted I come back to work exactly two weeks after my maternity leave ended which happened to be on a Friday. I thought it was a little ridiculous to start back on a Friday but it turned out it wasn't.

My first day back to work was a disaster. I felt as green as an intern the first day out of medical school. Just six weeks before the hospital had been my turf, but now I could barely remember where the bathrooms were.

My chief accomplishment on my first day back to work was making it home again in one piece. Luckily I then had the whole weekend to recover. The next week happened to be Christmas week and our clinic went on a half-day holiday schedule. Two weeks later, when we resumed our normal operations, I was back up to speed on the job.

I liked this gradual transition back to work so well that I planned something similar with my second baby. This time we knew what we were doing so I went back to work about five weeks after my baby was born.

I again came back to work on a Friday and kept my schedule light for a couple of weeks. I didn't work half days this time, but I also did not go out of my way to let people know I was back. Everyone had gotten used to my not being around so I let them carry on as they were until they figured out I was back. This took a couple of weeks.

WHAT SHOULD YOU TELL YOUR BOSS about breastfeeding? Tell him doctors recommend four to six weeks minimum time away from work after a baby is born and a gradual return to full work levels "like someone would have after surgery or a heart attack."

If you don't want to say any more than that, you do not have to. My boss was a middle-aged man with three teenage boys. I knew he wouldn't relate to what I was doing so I didn't waste time trying to explain it to him.

Modern breastfeeding such as I describe really has no impact on the workplace. We don't need special facilities or special breaks to breastfeed, and we don't run home every time our babies get hungry.

We are no more limited or tied down than any other workers. The idea that breastfeeding means that a mother and her baby cannot be separated is incorrect. If anyone at work seems to have that idea, tell them it just doesn't apply to what you are doing.

BABYSITTING has to be arranged before you can go back to work. Your options are to have someone come into your home, take your baby to someone else's home, or take your baby to a day care center. For babies under a year and a half I think the first two options are preferable because your baby will get more individualized attention that way.

You want someone to care for your baby who is reliable, trustworthy, safety-conscious, and who loves kids. Ask your friends and co-workers if they can recommend anyone. Call your city or county government to ask for a list of approved child care providers in your area. Ask any potential babysitters for references and talk to all of them!

I called the social services agency in California and was sent a list of all approved child care providers in my zip code area. First, I went by each house and crossed off any that were on very busy streets or just didn't look right.

Then I called the people on the list. Many said they had no room for infants. (This is usually the hardest age group to find sitting for because the states allow one babysitter to take care of more toddlers than infants.)

When someone said she could take an infant, I asked to come right over for an interview. I asked how long she had been babysitting, why she was babysitting, how long she had lived where she was, how many other children she took care of, and how long most children stayed with her.

I also asked what hours she would sit, whether she would take care of sick children, whether she was available on weekends or in the evening, how much she charged, and whether she smoked or had pets. I watched how she acted with my baby and whether my baby seemed to respond to her or not. Then I asked for a tour of the house.

The first lady I talked to was dressed in her housecoat and slippers at one in the afternoon. The soap operas were on and all the shades were pulled. A gigantic dog raced around the house, and the lady seemed to be ignoring an older baby who obviously wanted out of a play pen. This lady seemed nice and friendly enough, but I knew after I left that I did not want to go back to her house.

The gut feelings I got with the woman I ended up hiring were entirely different. Her house was more friendly, open and light. She had a fenced-in play area in back. She seemed enthusiastic and seemed to enjoy what she was doing. I liked the way she held and talked to my baby.

I called all her references, including some parents she said had enrolled their children in preschool and were no longer bringing them to her house. Their comments struck the same chord as my visit to her house had. After sleeping on it a couple of days, I felt good about the decision and hired her.

MY MOTHER DID NOT COME down when my first daughter was born. We asked her instead to come help when I went back to work, and I found that much more valuable. She stayed about a month and was most helpful.

By that time we had worked out our routines around the house so Mother was not in anyone's way. And it smoothed my transition back to work because neither I nor my husband had to pack up the baby and drop her off on the way to work right away.

When my mother went out during the day she left Sarah with our sitter and I picked her up on the way home from work. By the time Mother left we were used to our new routine and were able to get the baby to the sitter's house and ourselves to work on time without a hitch.

My husband usually dropped Sarah off in the morning and I picked her up at night so we could nurse as soon as we got home.

If you do not have the luxury of a transition period like this, practice more dry runs with your sitter before the big back-to-work day arrives.

YOU WILL NOTICE SOME CHANGES in your milk supply as you go back to work. *First,* expect an overall drop in the total amount of milk you make. With my babies I was able to save about seven ounces of milk a day less after going back to work than I had before.

Second, your milk supply will decrease a little through the work week. You will have less milk on Friday than you did on Monday, but extra nursing naps on the weekends will bring this right back up.

This slight up and down pattern is very stable and can go on indefinitely. It does not affect your baby because he will drink a steady amount of milk for your sitter regardless of what your milk supply does.

TAKE ANOTHER BABYMOON as you go back to work. For the first month or so keep things simple and curtail outside activities. Eat simply and let someone else worry about cleaning house. Spend as much time with your baby as you can when you are together for this transition period and then you can expand your comfort zone again.

THERE ARE SEVERAL OPTIONS for feeding your baby while you are working. If you work near where your baby stays, you can get together for a noontime nursing session. Many workers jog over the lunch hour so there is no reason why you can't have lunch with your baby if you want to.

Our sitter lived ten minutes from work so I went to her house at noon to nurse my first baby for several months. I liked dropping in at various times to see what was going on, and it was a pleasant pause in the middle of the day.

When I was on call in the evenings, my husband found it easier to bring Sarah to the hospital for a private feeding in my call room than to try to get her to take a bottle for supper.

It was somewhat inconvenient to go over to my sitter's house at noon so I did not bother to do this with our second child. Instead I stayed at work and collected milk with the technique I describe in the next chapter.

When you are tired of saving breast milk, or if your work takes you away from your family for considerable periods of time, let your babysitter supplement your breast milk with formula or solids. You can maintain a stable enjoyable nursing relationship for as long as you want to on this basis.

Finally, you will be minimizing the need for breast milk feedings while you are away by feeding your baby frequently when you are together. This is called Reverse Cycle Feeding and is the best kept secret of successful breastfeeding working women. It is explained in Chapter Ten.

REMEMBER THESE KEY POINTS FOR A SUCCESSFUL RETURN TO WORK:

FIRST, *build up a breast milk supply* in your freezer for your sitter to give your baby as needed. You will learn how to do this in the next chapter.

SECOND, *feed your baby frequently while you are together* so he won't be very hungry while you are apart, as discussed in Chapter Ten.

THIRD, *think about your priorities* and learn to *spend your time* as *carefully* as if it were gold, because time is the most precious asset you have. We will talk about priorities and time management in Chapter Eleven.

FOURTH, *expand your comfort zones* so that you become able to do whatever you want without stressing your nursing relationship.

FIFTH, *locate a babysitter you trust*, and practice leaving your baby with her so you will be ready for that first day of work.

SIXTH, *return to work on a Friday*, and keep a light schedule for the first few weeks. Explain to your boss that doctors recommend four to six weeks minimum time at home with a new baby "just like convalescence from surgery or a heart attack."

FINALLY, *take another babymoon* as you go back to work, where you let other things go and spend as much time with your baby as you can when you're together.

When you have been back to work a month, you will have made it past the greatest challenge to your breastfeeding relationship and will be a world-class breastfeeding expert. Enjoy your success!

9

Meals in Minutes: The Easy Way to Save Milk

If you know someone who has collected breast milk for her baby to drink later, I can almost guarantee she did not think it was very easy or very successful.

THERE ARE TWO CHOICES for saving breast milk, *mechanical* and *by-hand methods*. Our society is technologically oriented, so many gadgets have been developed that are supposedly useful in the saving of breast milk. Most of them are not.

Hand-held breast pumps are frequently recommended, but I don't know anyone who ever got one of them to work. Electric breast pumps are expensive and hard to find.

All breast pumps are somewhat hard to clean, and all can be, as Dr. Ruth Lawrence calls them, "instruments of torture."

Most breastfeeding books and articles describe an old-fashioned technique for collecting breast milk called **MANUAL EXPRESSION**. It was dreamed up by male physicians who obviously never had the opportunity to practice what they preached, and it should have been called "manual labor," because it is such hard work. You can spend hours and not get much for your efforts except chafed skin and sore breasts.

The reason all these ways to save milk are so ineffective is that they are *barking up the wrong tree.* They are all trying to suck or force milk out of the breasts, and as we know, that does not work very well. As we learned in Chapter One, let-down must occur for the breasts to be emptied.

IF LET-DOWN OCCURS *it is easy to save milk,* and you don't need a mechanical gadget to do so. *If let-down doesn't occur nothing happens.*

The only reliable way to get let-down started is by direct stimulation of the nipples, since it is the nerves in the nipples that start the let-down reflex.

There are two ways to get the necessary nipple stimulation to initiate let-down. *Your baby can do it* for you as he nurses or *you can do it by hand.* I collected milk frequently from one breast while my first baby nursed at the other. This is a easy and reliable method for beginners.

DISPOSABLE PLASTIC BOTTLES made for formula-feeding are ideal for collecting, freezing and feeding breast milk. These presterilized bags come on tear-off rolls of one hundred, and are used with a special holder that is ideal for saving milk because it has a wider mouth than regular baby bottles.

Evenflo, Playtex, Gerber and others make disposable bottle systems, and all their parts are interchangable.

You do not need the nipple and ring to collect milk, just the hard plastic holder and the roll of plastic bags. I kept a roll of bags and a holder at home and another set at work, along with a beach towel, a roll of masking tape, a marker, some paper cups, and some bread sack twist-ties.

I installed a plastic bag on the bottle holder according to the directions on the box. After collecting my milk, I took the plastic bag out of the holder, twisted the top and fastened it like I would a bread sack. Then I placed it upright in a paper cup and labeled it with the date.

The milk was then ready for the refrigerator if I thought it would be fed in the next two days, or for the freezer if I wanted to keep it indefinitely. With every bag of milk labeled by date, we were always able to use the oldest milk first.

WHEN YOUR BABY HELPS you save milk you generally collect from one side while your baby nurses at the other. Wash both your hands with soap and water, and fix a collecting bottle. Sit down in a comfortable chair (I used a rocking chair so I could rest my arms on the chair arms and easily wipe off any spills or spray droplets). Tuck a towel in under your nursing bra to catch drips.

Take your baby to the breast. As he stimulates let-down, pick up your collecting bottle and hold it near your other nipple. Gently squeeze and release the dark-skinned areola around your nipple. This will compress the milk sacs and pump milk from your breast.

fig. 9-1: HOW TO COLLECT MILK WHILE NURSING.

When your hand gets tired, rest. I generally did about twenty squeezes, then rested and repeated.

(If you want to do some preparation for breastfeeding before your baby is born, practice gently squeezing something with your thumbs and fingertips to build up the number of repititions you can do before getting tired. This would probably be more useful than nipple preparation exercises. Neither is required.)

Since my second baby threw up every time I tried to feed her sitting up, I could not conveniently save breast milk while she nursed. (It is possible to collect milk while nursing lying down, but gravity works against you and it isn't very restful.)

I got in the habit with Susan of collecting milk first while she was still asleep, and then enjoying a lengthy lying-down nursing session afterwards. Overall, I liked this arrangement better, and it really built up my milk supply.

TO SAVE MILK WHEN YOUR BABY ISN'T HELPING, first learn how to stimulate your let-down reflex yourself. A good time to experiment with this is during your sitz baths after you get home.

The moist heat in the bathtub sets the stage for let-down and provides lubrication. Use both hands to stimulate both nipples at once. I used the flat parts of my fingers and the palms of my hands to rub up and down on the nipples and surrounding aroela.

I see no point in massaging the entire breasts as is often recommended because you can easily hurt yourself, and the nerve endings you need to stimulate are in the nipple area, not in the breasts themselves.

EXPERIMENT until you find out what works well for you, and then practice it. If your husband and you want, he can become involved in learning how to stimulate let-down. But figure out how to do it yourself, too, because he isn't going to be around most of the time when you need to collect milk.

After you know what it takes to trigger your let-down reflex, locate the area where the milk sacs are in you, and practice squeezing there until you can effectively keep your milk flowing.

(In most women, the milk sacs are located under the line where their skin color changes from dark-skinned aroela to regular-colored breast. Some women have the darker skin over half of their breasts. In these women, the milk sacs are probably closer to the nipples than where the skin color changes.)

When you are good at letting down and keeping the milk flowing, reach for a bottle and collect some milk. You won't fill up the bag like turning on a water faucet. The first few squirts look mighty lonesome in the bottom of the bag so there's a bit of a psychological turn-off at this point that you have to overcome.

Relax. Tell yourself what a great job you are doing. The first few times you will be successful if you get this far without losing your enthusiasm. You don't have to save any milk yet. Just get a little in the bottle, pat yourself on the back, and stop. When you are comfortable doing all this graduate out of the bathtub and save some breast milk.

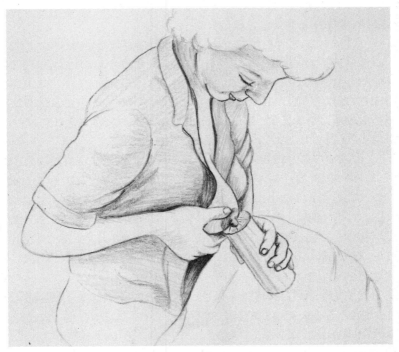

fig. 9-2: HOW TO COLLECT MILK WHEN BY YOURSELF.

To save milk when your baby isn't there, stimulate let-down yourself, and collect milk from both sides. Wash your hands with soap and water, and bring a cup of hot water for lubrication. Tuck a towel under your nursing bra to catch drips, and let down both flaps. Then stimulate let-down and start collecting milk.

WITH A GOOD LET-DOWN you will find yourself collecting milk at a rate of an ounce a minute or so, which certainly beats the one ounce per half-hour pace I managed with the manual expression technique!

After a few minutes the flow will taper off. You can probably restimulate the nipples to get another strong let-down at this point. I could invariably stimulate two let-downs per collecting session, and had my bag as full as I could get it in five to ten minutes.

Even though I couldn't stimulate any more let-downs myself, my baby could. After I had saved a meal she would take the breast and nurse happily and successfully. I would feel weak let-down sensations as she nursed, and she was able to empty the breasts far more completely than I could.

SAVE MILK BEFORE YOUR BABY NURSES to build up your milk supply and fill your freezer with breast milk. I was never able to successfully collect any milk just after my baby had nursed because all the let-downs seemed to be used up and had to be regenerated.

The only times you will not be able to collect breast milk effectively are just after your baby has nursed and when you can't let down. *If for some reason you cannot relax and let down don't try to force it.* Believe me, it does not work, and you will only end up feeling frustrated and like a failure.

YOU DON'T HAVE TO BE PERFECT to be effective. If you see things are not working out this time, quit while you are ahead and try again later.

Inability to let down is like inability to achieve an erection in men. It is going to happen now and then, especially while you are learning. But it does not mean that you are impotent unless you think you are. The fact that you had a baby means you have the right biological equipment for making milk and letting down. Practice and nurture things along, and you will do just fine.

SAVE MILK TWO OR THREE TIMES A DAY for two to four weeks before going back to work. This will give you a freezer milk bank sufficient to last about a month even if you do nothing else.

Save milk once a day at home and once a day at work for another month or two. Then, all you really need to do is collect some milk once a day at work to prevent uncomfortable swelling.

At some point you won't need to collect milk at all unless you want to, because your breasts will no longer be achy full at the end of the day even when you don't save milk at noon.

I liked my milk-saving breaks at work. They took only fifteen to twenty minutes, and gave me a chance to regroup for the second half of the day.

I rotated through a different department every
month after my first baby was born, as part of my
Internal Medicine training. Some months I had my
own office where I could lock the door and collect
milk privately at noon. Other times I saved milk in
the women's room.

Some of the time I had access to a refrigerator
used only by a few reliable people to store their
lunches. I left my breast milk in the freezer there
with no worry.

Other months the nearest refrigerator was on a
busy hospital ward where people came and went all
the time, with no sense of security. I had a
persistent nightmare that some new nurse's aide
was pouring urine in the wrong bag by mistake, so
I decided to make sure my breast milk was really
safe. I got a lockable box and put it in the freezer
with my name on it. That way I knew my milk was
untouched until I took it home.

I TOOK BREAST MILK HOME FROM WORK
in an insulated baby bottle bag. If the milk was still
liquid I left it in the paper cup and made sure it
didn't tip over. If it was frozen it didn't matter
what position it travelled in.

We took frozen milk to our babysitter six or
seven bags at a time in an insulated lunch bag. Any
sort of cooler, thermos or ice cream bag would also
work. If your commute isn't longer than a trip to
the grocery store your milk will stay cold enough
without any special bags.

YOU CAN FREEZE all your milk and use the oldest milk first. Or you can leave today's milk with your babysitter for tomorrow's use. I found it more convenient to freeze it all and rotate stock, and I didn't feel forced to produce on any given day if I didn't want to.

If your freezer keeps ice cream hard (or has a temperature of five degrees Fahrenheit or less), your breast milk will be good for at least six months. If your freezer can only keep ice cream soft, store your milk in the center of the freezer (where it is the coldest), and plan to use it within three months.

Fresh breast milk can be stored safely in the refrigerator for up to forty-eight hours.

TELL YOUR SITTER TO DISCARD any part of a bottle your baby starts but does not finish, just like you would formula. Do not attempt to feed it later because this might give your baby infectious diarrhea, a condition very unusual in breastfed babies.

FROZEN BREAST MILK CAN BE THAWED out at room temperature for a few hours, or in the refrigerator over night. As long as there is still ice in the bag, the milk is very cold and safe. The bag can then be held under hot running tap water or dipped in a pan of boiling water to bring to feeding temperature.

Breast milk and formula should not be heated up in a microwave, because vitamins are destroyed.

IT IS NORMAL for breast milk to separate as it stands because it is not homogenized. You will see a fatty layer on top and skim milk on the bottom. Shake the bottle before feeding to remix the milk.

The first milk that comes out of your breasts is thin and watery blue. The later milk has the most fat content. If you let down well and collect milk easily, it will have a nice fat layer upon standing.

REMEMBER THESE KEY POINTS:

LET-DOWN MUST OCCUR to save milk effectively. The most reliable way to get let-down started is by direct stimulation of the nipples. If for some reason you cannot let down, stop trying to save milk and come back to it later. Good times to collect milk are before or during a feeding, or when separated from your baby. You cannot save milk effectively right after a nursing session.

DISPOSABLE NURSING BOTTLES made for formula-feeding are ideal for collecting, freezing, and feeding breast milk.

BREAST MILK WILL KEEP in a good freezer for many months. It keeps in the refrigerator for forty-eight hours. Any breastmilk left over after a feeding should be thrown away to prevent illness.

Now that you know how to stimulate let-down, you'll be saving breast milk meals in minutes. In the next chapter we will see how to minimize the amount of breast milk your baby will need by using *reverse cycle feeding.*

10

Reverse Cycle Feeding: A Working Mother's Most Powerful Secret

When our first baby was three months old we ran out of extra breast milk in the freezer. From then on whatever milk I collected one day was fed the next, which put me under pressure to perform.

Back then I didn't know that the secret to saving milk was stimulating the nipples until let-down occurs. I tried everything I could think of to get my milk flowing when my baby wasn't there: everything from "thinking of baby" and "using moist heat," to self-hypnosis and positive thinking. None of these worked reliably.

I tried manual expression, squeezing my breasts with both hands as I moved from my chest wall toward the nipple. This sometimes hurt my breasts and made my skin look like coarse sandpaper. But it usually didn't produce much milk.

Our second baby was born hungry and wanted to nurse all the time. I thought this was wonderful because I knew her lusty nursing would stimulate a bountiful milk supply.

I wanted to make and save all the extra breast milk I could so my freezer would be loaded when I went back to work. I didn't want to run out of extra milk at three months again.

About this time I read the experiment where mother rabbits' nipples were numbed with xylocaine. This blocked the let-down reflex. The baby rabbits nursed but got nothing until the effects of the xylocaine wore off and sensation returned to the nipples.

THIS WAS THE SECRET I had been looking for -- the key to saving milk. I began to use direct nipple stimulation before saving milk and my success rate improved greatly. I consistently got much more milk in much less time, and didn't hurt my breasts doing it.

With Susan nursing so vigorously and the new-found secret to milk-saving success I easily saved six to seven ounces of milk three times a day even after I went back to work!

Every time my freezer got full, I took milk to our sitter's house. With our first baby she was always saying, "We need some more milk." This time she would say, "Goodness! What are we going to do with all this milk?" I don't have to tell you which question I liked better.

BUT I STILL HAD A PROBLEM. By three months of age Susan was drinking twenty-one ounces of breast milk a day while I was at work. And I was frankly getting tired of saving milk.

I was about to give up, use up the breast milk left in the freezer and buy formula. Then I read how some mothers in Los Angeles were nursing their babies frequently during the evenings and at night, so that the babies wouldn't be hungry during the day. Since this is opposite from how babies are usually fed, it is called *reverse cycle feeding*.

REVERSE CYCLE FEEDING worked like magic for me. At three months of age Susan was no longer eating at night. She often went from eight PM until five the next morning without a meal.

I immediately added several feedings. I made sure that I fed her when I went to bed, even though she wasn't stirring. I was still waking up several times a night, so every time I woke up for one reason or another, I took Susan to the breast.

Still asleep, she nursed avidly whenever the breast was offered. After a ten-minute quickie she was back in her bassinet and I back in dreamland. With essentially no effort, I increased the number of night time feedings by four or five.

THE RESULTS WERE PHENOMENAL. From then on Susan went to our sitter's house stuffed. She refused to eat or drink anything until about one PM. Then she would take seven ounces but would not eat again until I picked her up in the evening.

I quit saving breast milk altogether except over the noon hour for my comfort, and we didn't run out of breast milk in the freezer until Susan was one year old!

The more your baby nurses while you are together, the less milk you'll need to leave for your sitter to feed when you're gone.

THIS IS A SIMPLE PLAN once you think of it, and it works beautifully. But it seems to go against childrearing advice that emphasizes getting your baby to "sleep through the night." (This is the anthem of bottle-feeding parents who are sick of fixing bottles in the middle of the night.)

Actually, reverse cycle feedings don't keep babies from sleeping through the night because nursing babies are asleep for night-time feedings, anyway. If your baby has problems being awake at night, review how to reset his biological time clock on page 65.

AS YOUR BABY STARTS TAKING SOLIDS, gradually taper off the night time feedings as he increases his table foods. By the time he is one year old your baby will be eating three meals a day at the table like the rest of the family does.

USE FREQUENT FEEDINGS when you are with your baby so he won't be very hungry when you are away. That way you don't have to save much milk, and you both get to continue an enjoyable breastfeeding experience.

11

Where Do I
Get Enough Time?

My husband spent five years talking me into having children. He wanted them. I didn't. I was afraid I would be stuck and would not have any time for myself.

TIME FOR SELF is a major concern of all new mothers. I don't think you have to give up things that are important to you in order to experience the joys of parenthood. But you do have to know what is important to you and stick to your priorities.

You can have it all -- time for yourself, enjoyment of family, and a career. This is not any harder to do if you are breastfeeding than if you were bottle feeding your baby. But it won't happen automatically. It takes determination, flexibility, practice and a plan. You have got to set limits and stick to them.

It's like the video game *Pigs in Space,* where Miss Piggie has been jettisoned from the star ship Swinetrek and is trying to get back before the ship disappears from the screen.

She has to travel through an asteroid belt of slithering spaghetti and meatballs. Each time she gets smacked by this mess she is bounced further away from the ship. Only with persistence and skill can she dodge the distractions and make it to her goal.

You have to be equally persistent and skillful to make it to your goals. *No one is born with great goal-setting skills. Everyone gets more skillful the more they play the game.*

There will be days when the meatballs come hard and fast, your timing is off, and you take direct hit after direct hit. The only redeeming feature about days like this is that they cannot last forever.

SET YOUR PRIORITIES and keep your goals clearly in mind, and days where you are totally distracted from your goals won't even be common.

Priorities. What's important to you? Only you can answer that. You are here for some purpose and only you can determine what that is. I think you need time for yourself to determine your direction in life. When things seem most confusing this need is greatest.

You also need time for yourself to play, relax, and rejuvenate. You're not much good to anyone else if you are so burned out you hate everything you are doing. No one can work twenty-four hours a day, seven days a week, week after week and be half as effective as when they are fresh.

You have got to take care of yourself for the long haul or you won't be around for the long haul. It is better to build rest and relaxation into your schedule every day than to get it all in one lump sum when you totally collapse.

YOU ALSO NEED TIME TO PLAN, to think about what you are doing and why. Do you really want to be doing everything you are doing now? What is most important to you? What do you want to get done first? What is optional? What's not worth doing at all?

Are there easier ways to accomplish the things you want to get done? Can anything be done faster or more effectively? Is there any way to make things more fun? *If you don't decide how to invest your time, other people will!*

A GOOD TIME FOR DAILY PLANNING SESSIONS is during long lying-down nursing sessions before and after work and on milk-saving breaks during the day.

An hour a day spent planning and thinking about where you are going and how you want to get there is the best investment of time you will ever make. You will be astonished at what you can accomplish if you set your goals and spend an hour a day thinking about how to reach them.

I SAW A HUNTER shoot into a herd of antelope one time on my father's farm in Wyoming. Twenty animals raced for the horizon. Four stayed behind.

A doe had been hit in the shoulder and was trying to make it to the nearest fence on three feet. A buck and twin fawns stayed with her and stood their ground as the hunter approached. That's family: together in the face of death while the rest of the herd heads for the hills.

Although we do not feel the intensity of bonding to our families every day, those bonds are there. And they are worth plenty. Even if things aren't going well with our families, at least we know what is wrong with them, and that's more than we can say about strangers. *There is no better place to invest time and energy than with our families.*

YOUR FIRST PRIORITY in life is to yourself, and then to your family. But let's look for a minute at where the demands on your time are coming from. Most of the urgent, "do it now" demands do not come from you or your family.

You don't knock on your door every five minutes demanding to be seen right now. Your family doesn't ring your phone off the hook wanting today's reports done yesterday. Most of these meatballs are coming from areas less important to you than yourself and your family!

LET'S DISTINGUISH between URGENT and IMPORTANT. Very few of the important things in life are urgent, meaning that they must be taken care of right away. (When my membranes ruptured and I started having contractions every three minutes, that was one time.)

MOST OF THE IMPORTANT THINGS IN LIFE ARE NOT URGENT. Like making out your will, saving for the future, or stopping smoking. (If you do smoke, how about stopping now for your own benefit as well as your baby's?)

MOST OF THE THINGS THAT SEEM URGENT ARE NOT VERY IMPORTANT. *Just because someone is standing in front of you with an outstretched hand doesn't mean his request is more important than your goals and priorities.*

One thing I am proud I accomplished in my two years as a doctor in North Carolina is that I set up a stop-smoking program. Time spent preventing disease is far more beneficial than time spent locking the barn door after the horse has escaped.

Even though I knew preventing disease was important, it took me over a year to get the first stop-smoking group set up. No one was pounding my door down demanding a stop-smoking group now! But that group was more important than many of the urgent demands people did knock on my door with day after day after day.

I finally dodged enough meatballs to make this goal a reality. Now I am eager to continue helping people stay well, and I have other preventive medicine projects in mind.

I can see that if I don't keep my priorities straight in medicine, my time will be totally dominated by other people's urgent demands, and I may never achieve some of the things I feel are really important.

BUSY WORK wastes as much time as urgent but not important things. If you can control these two categories of time use, you will have plenty of time for yourself and for doing the things you think are important.

Busy work is anything that makes us feel like we have accomplished something when we really haven't. Some busywork we learned from our role models, but the rest we have developed on our own. Like folding sheets to take upstairs to unfold and make the bed. Or cleaning off a desk by putting everything on the bookcase. Or vacuuming the guest bedroom every week when no one has used it for nine months.

Fight back against busy work in the kitchen with speed-minded cookbooks like *The 60-Minute Gourmet* or *Fifteen-Minute Meals.*

ENLIST YOUR HUSBAND in the war against housework busy work. You were probably trained to "do" housework, while your husband was probably spared this education. Therefore, his mind hasn't been cluttered with as many time-wasting housekeeping routines, so he might be quicker than you at spotting what really needs to be done and getting it done.

Most men won't leap forward volunteering to do housework. They probably will never show great interest in this area. But they do not have to be perfect to be effective, and now that they are fathers, it is time for them to do their fair share if they have not already been doing so.

Since you are breastfeeding, your husband has a wonderful situation at home compared to what equal-opportunity bottle-feeding dads have. Since you are doing all the feeding that he would otherwise be helping with, he should agree that it's fair for him to assume more household duties. If he is reluctant, let him change all the dirty diapers for a while when he is home.

WHEN YOUR HUSBAND AGREES to do some housework, leave him alone. It may be best to actually leave the house while he does it until you learn how to look the other way and bite your tongue. I guarantee he won't do everything the way you've been taught it should be done. If you stay around while he cleans house, you are likely to get into an argument over technique and forget it 's the results that count.

When we were medical students neither one of us gave housework a high priority. When things got really messy, Wendell would invite someone over to eat as motivation to clean up. He always cooked for company in those days, because his ego wasn't as fragile as mine. If the meal flopped it didn't bother him like it would have bothered me.

The first few times we invited people over for supper we were just about at each other's throats arguing about the housework by the time the guests arrived. Finally, one day I said, "You invited them: you clean up. I'm going to the library."

He said, "Great. Don't come back before five."

I got back fifteen minutes before the guests arrived. Wendell was happy as a lark, calm and collected with a great meal cooking. And the place looked beautiful. It was a little hard for me to swallow, but he had done it all by himself, in less time than we usually spent together, and the results were outstanding.

After that, we set up a Saturday morning field day where we washed clothes and picked up the major debris. Our housekeeping has gotten better as time goes by. By the time our firstborn reached the crawling stage we were organized enough to be vacuuming the floor once a week. (Whatever else happened, we didn't want Sarah to be eating paper clips!)

The most important thing about our Saturday morning field day is that it ends at noon and we get the rest of the weekend to play. *We do a better job with housework if we reward ourselves after it is done than if we devote all weekend to putting it off.*

FIGURE OUT WAYS TO PREVENT HOUSEWORK whenever possible. Five minutes preventing a cleaning job is worth an hour having to do one. We load the dishwasher as we are cooking before the food dries on, and take our muddy shoes off at the door. We have carpet sweepers and cleaning supplies within easy reach upstairs and downstairs and find it easier to grab something for a quick clean-up as needed than to slave over everything later.

Since we are all away from home on weekdays, our house does not get brutalized every day. Preventive measures, five-minute touch-ups, and Saturday morning field days give us a house of acceptable cleanliness and tidiness without wasting a lot of our time.

AT WORK I fight busy work better than most of my male colleagues. Their egos are tied up in "working," while I want to get my work *done* and get out of there as quickly as possible.

There is no correlation between the number of hours spent at work and the quality or amount of work accomplished. Work expands to fill the time allowed for it. Just because bachelors hang around the office after work to kill time doesn't mean you should imitate their bad work habits.

We went to medical school in Salt Lake City, Utah. Our devout Mormon classmates reserved Sundays and Wednesday evenings for church activities. Our professors loved to schedule exams for Monday or Thursday mornings. That killed the weekend for most of us, who studied up until the moment of the test.

But our devout Mormon classmates closed their books Saturday night and did not study on Sunday. They did as well as the rest of us did on the tests, proving that you do not have to study all the time to get through medical school.

The superstar interns and residents I saw during my training were usually among the first people to leave the hospital each day. Those still bumbling around the wards at ten PM when they were not on call were usually still trying to figure out what was going on.

When we were interns, I lived, ate, slept, and breathed medicine. We were at the hospital most of the time, and I read medical journals at home. The first nine months of my residency training my husband was at sea on a Naval cruise. I had a hectic schedule, and often didn't get home before nine at night.

When Wendell got home from his cruise, I drew the line. I decided that I would never take work home with me again. And, unless there was a true emergency, I would go home by five or six PM. If some things didn't get done, they would just have to wait until the next day.

Guess what happened? By setting limits I got more efficient than I had been before. And I'm still getting better at accomplishing more in the same amount of time. If I had not drawn the line between work and home, I would still probably be wasting my evenings reading medical journals.

One of the best decisions we made when our children got to preschool age was to pick a school with fairly short hours. That forced at least one of us to go to work later than we otherwise might have, and made at least one of us leave work in time to pick the kids up.

Do not let your job take over your whole life. Draw the line and don't step over it. Not only will you have more time for yourself and your family, but in the long run you will also become better at your job because you will have learned to be more efficient.

WHAT ABOUT "WASTED" TIME? Would we get more done if we did not "goof off?" I don't think so. *Anything you truly feel good about afterwards is probably good for you.* (If you smoke, you don't truly feel good about smoking...)

REST AND RELAXATION TIME is essential to keep you going. If you don't get everything done that is important, do not take away your fun time. Ax some of the busy work, and don't give so much time to urgent things that are not very important. Go ahead and enjoy your fun time. It really is not wasted.

We all need fun time for rest and relaxation to avoid burnout and to reward ourselves for jobs well done. Play is fun and it's good for you. One of the benefits of having kids is that you won't look foolish playing with any toy you want as long as a child is present as chaperone.

WE WILL MEET OUR GOALS if we get done the important things in life even when they are not urgent. To do this we need to minimize time spent on busy work and the urgent demands that really aren't important.

Time is the stuff of which life is made. We all have exactly the same amount given to us each day. We can't control all of our time. In fact, with our jobs and the responsibilities of daily living, other people will probably be dictating how we spend most of our time.

YOU WILL PROBABLY BE ABLE to wrestle only a few hours a day to do with as you will. But if you use it wisely, you can have time for it all: self, family, career, and fun. Set your priorities and think so you can manage your time effectively. And enjoy your new baby.

12

Crisis!

Overcoming challenges or potential crises is part of what makes breastfeeding so exhilirating. As you nurse your baby you'll face a variety of situations that will make you wonder whether you've got what it takes to breastfeed successfully. (Ninety-five percent of all new mothers do so you probably do, too.)

Every time you overcome a potential crisis your self-esteem rises and you will feel invincible. If for some reason you don't meet the challenge, however, you may risk developing breastfeeding impotence.

BREASTFEEDING IMPOTENCE is where a mother comes to believe that she can't nurse her baby when in fact she can. It is more easily prevented than cured and is basically a confidence game. *If you believe you can do it, you almost certainly can breastfeed your baby. If you doubt your abilities, you may have trouble. You can't lose your milk, but you can doubt it away.*

No one would tell a young man, "Don't worry, there's always artificial insemination," if he has trouble performing sexually. Yet breastfeeding mothers are frequently advised to give up and formula-feed every time a little problem comes up.

FIVE BIOLOGICAL FUNCTIONS are related to the female sex: sexual intercourse, menstrual cycles, pregnancy, childbirth, and nursing a baby. The first and last of these are by far the most fun, and most women want to experience the full range of their sexual natures.

Suggestions that we shouldn't bother trying to nurse our babies are as inappropriate and outdated as the advice that we should be happy if our husbands are satisfied and should not expect to achieve orgasm ourselves. Women are just not buying that line any more. We shouldn't believe that nursing our babies is unimportant either.

THE FIRST STEP TO OVERCOMING A CRISIS is to stick with the right crowd. Keep the faith. *Remember your breastfeeding goals.* Do not listen if people tell you you should give up and go to formula feeding. Lay people have no business advising you how to feed your baby.

Your doctor will be happy if your baby regains his birth weight by two weeks of age. Since you are nursing frequently and have set aside a babymoon period to learn how to nurse, your baby probably will have more than regained his birth weight by two weeks of age. *If he nurses frequently, seems satisfied, wets his diapers six or more times a day, and either has frequent bowel movements or massive ones, your baby is doing well.*

THE SECOND STEP to overcoming any nursing crisis you may face is to go back to square one. *Go back to your most basic comfort zone and regroup.* Take a nap with your baby at the breast in a quiet, comfortable babymoon setting. Things will always look better after you get some sleep.

THE THIRD STEP to managing breastfeeding crises is to *think*. Troubleshoot. Figure out what is going on and come up with a plan for surmounting the problem. Every time you overcome what could have been a breastfeeding disaster you will feel ten feet tall.

POTENTIAL CRISES as you breastfeed can be grouped into five categories: behavioral changes, supply and demand problems, situational changes, mechanical troubles, and "numbers" crises.

BEHAVIORAL CHANGES as your baby grows and develops can present breastfeeding challenges. A three-month old doesn't act the same as a newborn. As a tooth comes in, your baby may behave in some new and interesting ways. *All you have to do when your baby changes his behavior is to figure out an effective countermove.*

Between three and four months of age babies become interested in the world around them. This can be maddening to a nursing mother until she learns some new behaviors of her own. Women have actually given up and gone to formula feeding at three months because they didn't understand how easily behavioral changes can be handled.

One mother reported trouble with the cat when her baby was three months old. She liked to sit on the couch to nurse, and her cat liked to pace back and forth behind her. But at three months of age her baby became so interested in watching the cat go back and forth that he wouldn't stop to nurse. The mother finally started putting the cat outside before nursing and had no further difficulties.

Whatever behavioral changes your baby goes through he will always nurse in his sleep, and he will usually nurse in a dark quiet bedroom once all the distractions have been removed.

SUPPLY AND DEMAND problems are usually caused by growth spurts. *Any time your baby seems hungrier than usual, call it a growth spurt and let him nurse all he wants to.* Let him nurse all night long even if you are bone dry, and within a day or two you'll be experiencing another kind of supply and demand problem: what to do with all that extra milk. (Easy. Just put it in the freezer!)

SITUATIONAL CHANGES may lead to crises in breastfeeding. Some changes we plan for, like our return to work. Others may surprise us, like the need for emergency surgery. If you or your baby has to go into the hospital for some reason, don't panic. Explain to the staff that you are breastfeeding and work out visitation rights.

Freezer milk or formula can be used to fill in any gaps in what you can deliver, and your breasts can be emptied manually or with the hospital's breast pump if need be. Your baby will appreciate the reassurance of being nursed, and as soon as the crisis is past you can easily build your milk supply up again with frequent nursings as you would with any other supply and demand problem.

ADDING TO YOUR ACTIVITIES can stress your breastfeeding relationship. Your changing behavior may confuse your baby as much as his changing behavior confuses you.

I have *two rules of thumb* about adding to your activities as you breastfeed. I don't believe being "tied down" to a breastfeeding baby is good for either the baby or the mother. You both need to be doing what you want to be doing for this to be a beneficial relationship.

First, if you really want to do something, go ahead. Do it. You'll be frustrated if you don't, and that's not good for you or your baby. As long as you give your baby lots of nursing and cuddling before and afterwards, he won't get too upset.

Second, if for some reason you really don't want to do something, don't do it. Life is too short to do things that won't please you. Your baby is a perfect excuse to get out of things you don't want to do, because people expect you to be "confined" for awhile. (While you are getting off the hook this way, try to figure out why you feel obligated to do things you don't want to do in the first place, and work on that.)

GOING BACK TO WORK is a major potential crisis, and was discussed in Chapter Eight, "Staging Your Comeback: Planning the Return to Work."

WORK INVOLVING TRAVEL may result in situational crises. If you and your baby adapt, your breastfeeding relationship can continue even though you are gone quite a bit of the time. Some mothers take their babies with them. Others don't and express milk while they are away to maintain their milk production and for comfort.

One of my friends went on a trip for a week without her baby when he was five months old. He got formula and frozen breast milk, while she emptied her breasts as they filled up for comfort and to maintain her milk supply.

Her milk supply did decrease somewhat over the week, but her baby readily took the breast when she returned. Then a weekend babymoon restored her milk supply to previous levels.

We took our nursing babies along to medical meetings out of town. We took turns babysitting and attending the sessions. An ice-filled wash basin kept my collected breast milk safely for others to feed while I was away.

MECHANICAL PROBLEMS can precipitate a breastfeeding crisis. Most breastfeeding women will never get a plugged duct or mastitis, but if you do it's a potential crisis.

Mastitis is an inflammation or infection of the breast that occurs in breastfeeding women. It is best prevented by frequent emptying of your milk, just like bladder infections are best prevented by frequent emptying of the bladder. *Try not to go more than six to eight hours without nursing your baby or expressing milk or you will be at risk for developing mastitis.*

Mastitis occurred in the mother of a three month old breastfed baby who was "sleeping through the night." He didn't nurse at all between supper time and six in the morning. His mother always woke up with uncomfortably full breasts.

One morning she woke up with a red painful lump in her breast and a fever. Antibiotics and frequent nursing sessions cured the infection, but it would not have occurred if she had nursed around the clock.

Plugged ducts are a rare mechanical problem than can cause significant pain and put you at risk for mastitis. I was plagued by this problem for a year and a half until I learned about a change in my diet that cured it completely.

When my baby was five months old I noticed a small white spot on one of my nipples. A portion of that breast was full of milk and very tender.

As my baby nursed the tender area didn't empty. It became more uncomfortable as time went by.

I was told I had a plugged duct, and was advised to apply "moist heat" to open it up. It took awhile to figure out how to apply moist heat, but I finally dipped the nipple in a glass of hot water. (It's funny how sensitive nipples are to pinching and biting, but how comfortable they are in hot water.)

After a minute or two with my nipple in hot water, milk started squirting from the normal ducts. I had to press on the lump to get milk dribbling from the plugged duct. When my baby nursed the lump got a little smaller but it didn't go away.

The only time I found it useful to massage my breasts rather than the nipples was when I had a plugged duct. Stimulating the nipple and squeezing the milk sacs didn't empty the sore part of my breast because the duct was plugged.

So I massaged over the lump towards the nipple as my baby nursed. When I finally got enough back pressure built up the plug was forced out and the lump emptied.

The trouble was, this same duct kept plugging up over and over again. It gave me trouble for months until Sarah quit nursing. Then when my second baby was four weeks old it started to plug up again. For at least two months I didn't go more than three or four days without this duct being plugged up.

Then I read Dr. Ruth Lawrence's book where she talked about treating plugged ducts with low saturated fat diets. That was the key to solving my problem. I had been drinking more milk than usual, and had switched from one percent to whole milk while nursing.

I realized whole milk was very high in saturated fats so I switched back to one percent and quit trying to drink a quart a day. My ducts never plugged up again!

"NUMBERS" CRISES are usually pseudo-crises. They come about when someone thinks your baby is not measuring up to their yardstick of infant development. Breastfeeding is a quality experience with many dimensions that cannot be measured or weighed. But we live in a society that likes to measure and count, and it is amazing how many ways people try to keep score.

Friends, neighbors, grandparents, and doctors will all probably gauge your baby's progress by numbers of some sort. They will ask how often your baby nurses, how much he has gained, and how many times he "wakes up during the night."

Your first potential numbers crisis will be when your baby gets his two-week weight check. There are *three possible outcomes* here. *First*, your baby may have gained more than expected, in which case you will be congratulated for being a good nurser. (I expect most of my mothers will fall into this category.)

Second, your baby may have gained back to exactly his birth weight by the two week check. *All babies lose weight for awhile as they figure out how to eat, and if they are back to birth weight by two weeks they are doing well.*

(Bottle-fed babies may grow faster than your breastfed baby because they are basically overfed by big holes in bottle nipples and parents who try to stuff down that last half an ounce each feeding. The growth charts your pediatrician uses were based on information about bottle-fed babies, and may make your baby look "small." Don't pay any attention to what percentile your baby falls on. Just look to see that he stays on his own growth curve once he establishes it.)

Third, your baby may weigh less at two weeks than he did at birth. This would be unusual, and is the only time his weight should be of some concern. Work with your doctor carefully if this situation occurs, because you will want to make sure there is no health problem causing the poor weight gain, such as hypothyroidism in you or birth defects in your baby.

IF YOUR BABY'S A WEAK NURSER let your doctor know. Get him thinking about possible medical causes and *don't let him brush things off too quickly as "poor let-down" or "not enough time at the breast."*

Since babies are born "unfinished," they may have trouble with coordination until their nervous systems mature. Physical therapists trained to work with children can prescribe exercises to improve coordination in poorly sucking babies.

If your baby has physical problems, don't be too quick to abandon breastfeeding because if he has trouble nursing, he will probably also have trouble bottle-feeding until he gets older. There are ways you can supplement a poorly gaining baby with formula while continuing to breastfeed.

THE LACT-AID NURSING SUPPLEMENTER consists of a bag to hold formula, and narrow tubing that is taped near the mother's nipple so her baby can get formula as he nurses. If you need more information about a Lact-Aid or similar device, contact:

La Leche League International
9616 Minneapolis Avenue
Franklin Park, IL 60131
(312) 455-7730.

You can order a Lact-Aid from:

Lact-Aid International
P.O. Box 1066
Athens, TN 80206.

Most babies who use a Lact-Aid Supplementer outgrow their need for it as they mature and get to be better nursers.

BREASTFEEDING PROBLEMS can be viewed as crises or as challenges. Each time you successfully identify and solve a problem, your self-esteem heightens, and your pride will fuel continued breastfeeding success.

If you give up, you will feel like a failure.

REMEMBER THESE STEPS TO OVER-COMING BREASTFEEDING CRISES:

FIRST, *remember your breastfeeding goals.* Stick with what you said you would do.

SECOND, *go back to square one and regroup.* Take a nap with your baby at the breast in a quiet, comfortable babymoon setting. Things will always look better in the morning.

THIRD, *think.* Figure out what is going on and come up with a plan for surmounting the problem. If it's a behavioral problem, how can you change the setting? If it's a growth spurt, do you want to make up for it tonight or this weekend? If there is a situational change, how can you compensate for it with your baby? If it's a mechanical problem, do you need your doctor's help? If it's a "numbers" crisis, is it real or just a pseudo-crisis caused by other people being too numbers-oriented?

FINALLY, *decide on a plan of action.* Crises are challenges, and you have the knowledge and skills to overcome breastfeeding challenges.

13

How to Work With Your Doctor

My specialty is Internal Medicine -- I treat adults with medical problems. I haven't delivered a baby or doctored a sick child since medical school and my rotating internship. But because I have both received and dispensed it, I think I can tell you why Erma Bombeck says pediatric advice is some of the best comedy being written today.

Many pediatricians I know dislike adult medicine because they say people abuse their bodies for twenty to thirty years with alcohol, tobacco, the wrong foods, and lack of exercise and then want us to take care of the mess. I didn't like pediatrics because I seemed to spend half my time dispensing advice I knew nothing about.

I was the youngest child in my family. I babysat only twice in my entire life, and had never changed a diaper or fed a baby bottle until a gang of nurses cornered me during my internship and forced me to.

So when a mother would ask me what kind of diapers to buy or when to start feeding solids, I felt like saying, "Why are you asking me? I don't have any idea!"

But doctors in training can't keep saying "I don't know," so I listened to what residents and staff doctors told parents. If it seemed to get them off the hook, I tried it out the next time I was in a bind. Nothing builds confidence like success, so every time a mother seemed to accept my advice I felt less foolish giving it.

ALL BOARD-CERTIFIED pediatricians and family practitioners have been trained to diagnose and treat illnesses in children. They also emphasize preventive medicine and well child care, so they are good at checking your baby for proper growth and development, treating any illness that might occur, and nagging you to use car seats.

This is what your child's doctor is really there for, and *board certification means your doctor meets national standards in these areas.*

When it comes to child-rearing, however, the advice your doctor gives may be good or it may not be. Here there are no national standards, so the advice you get depends a lot on your doctor's own personal experience and the theories of those who trained him.

I'm not sure why Americans look to doctors for child-rearing advice. Europeans don't. I think the best practical child-rearing advice comes from people who rear children, and most male doctors don't presently fall into this category.

(I know a pediatrician who took his toddlers to a shopping mall once. He wandered off, forgot all about them, and drove home alone. Now his wife doesn't leave him with the kids unchaperoned.)

DON'T EXPECT YOUR DOCTOR to know anything about breastfeeding. We were all taught in medical school that "breast is best," and that all babies should be breastfed for the first year of life if possible.

But once we got out of the classroom into the real world of pediatric clerkships, we didn't hear much about breastfeeding any more. What we did hear was academic, not practical.

We discussed how many milliequivalents of potassium were in the various prepared formulas, and the rising pediatric stars always remembered the exact numbers. (I didn't, and I hated this kind of rounds.)

My pediatric attendings all loved numbers. They wanted to know how many ounces a baby was getting each feeding, and expected me to know how to calculate the number of kilocalories per day required for growth and for maintenance. But we didn't talk about how to get a baby to take the breast, or what to do about a teething crisis.

Remember that your doctor has been trained to evaluate growth and development, emphasize preventive medicine, and treat illnesses should they arise, but he is not a breastfeeding expert. Use him in his areas of expertise, and turn to breastfeeding experts for most of your breastfeeding advice.

GROWTH AND DEVELOPMENT will be the main item on your pediatrician's agenda for your baby's first year. His well baby checks are designed to turn up early clues to treatable and preventable disorders. The first year of life is the highest risk time of childhood, because it is when most birth defects show up.

Your pediatrician will be using growth charts and behavioral assessments to make sure your baby is developing normally. There is a broad range of normal for weights and behavioral milestones, so try not to fall into the common first-time parent trap of thinking your baby should be at the fiftieth percentile of everything. He won't be. Nobody's kid is.

Remember also that the growth charts your doctor uses were based on bottle-fed babies, who as a group gain weight faster than breastfed babies because they are relatively overfed. Breastfed babies as a group end up just as tall and heavy at two years of age as bottle-fed babies; they just gain weight at a slower, more steady pace.

YOUR BABY will pick out his own curve on the growth chart. As long as he stays on his own curve, he's doing well. If your baby drops off the curve on one visit, don't panic. It probably doesn't mean anything. All babies go up and down a little around an average as they grow, and length measurements tend to vary on growth charts more than weight measurements.

If your baby drops off his growth curve a little, treat him as if he is having a growth spurt and go back for a recheck when your doctor asks you to. Only if your baby persistently drops off his growth curve will further evaluation be necessary. Your doctor will have his agenda for such an evaluation. Refer back to Chapter 12 for yours.

BIRTH CONTROL may be on your agenda for discussion with your doctor. Here is an area where experts have looked at the same scientific evidence and come up with completely opposite conclusions.

Some experts say that if you nurse your baby frequently enough to totally supply his nutrition into the weaning period, you will be infertile for a long period of time.

Before formula was introduced to the Eskimos in Alaska, children there were born about two and a half years apart. Once bottle-feeding became common, this birth interval dropped to between twelve and fifteen months.

Whereas bottle-feeding mothers start having menstrual periods within weeks after their babies are born, breastfeeding mothers go an average of nine to twelve months before menses return, and less than six percent of new mothers ovulate before their first menstrual periods.

Sheila Kippley wrote a book about natural child spacing using the infertility of breastfeeding. She reported on the experiences of over a hundred women who followed her natural child spacing plan. These mothers didn't use pacifiers and didn't supplement with formula. They fed no solids and gave no liquids other than breast milk for the first five months. They used night-time feedings and lying-down nursing sessions.

The average length of time before these women began having menstrual periods again was fourteen months, and quite a number didn't resume menses until their babies were two years old or older.

I had my first period nine months after my first baby was born, and a year after the second baby. (Menstrual discomfort was the only thing I gave up to breastfeed my babies!) Because you will be comfort nursing, nursing at night, and using lying-down nursing, I expect you will enjoy a long menses-free interval, too.

YOU WILL HAVE TO DECIDE for yourself what degree of certainty you require for birth control and plan accordingly. For many people the major hurdle was becoming a parent in the first place, and they do plan on having another child sometime. If timing isn't critical for you, you may decide to rely on the relative infertility your breastfeeding gives you.

If you don't want to trust entirely to nature, you can use barrier methods, which in my opinion are safer than anything else available except abstinence and breastfeeding. When used all the time, barrier methods such as foam and condoms are as effective as birth control pills.

LOW-DOSE BIRTH CONTROL PILLS are often prescribed for breastfeeding women, because many doctors think they are safe. At least a dozen studies have appeared in the medical literature indicating their apparent safety, and none have appeared showing they are not safe.

Other doctors recommend you avoid using all types of birth control pills during breastfeeding for two reasons. First, they may decrease your milk supply slightly. (The older high-dose birth control pills definitely decreased milk supply.) Second, there is lingering concern that eventually harmful effects will be shown in the babies.

If you wish to use anything other than barrier methods or your natural infertility, talk to your doctor about it. If you decide to use the pill, plan on using other methods of birth control for at least two months. By then your milk will be firmly established, and you will be past all the hormonal changes of pregnancy that increase the risk of birth control pills causing blood clots or other problems.

IF YOU TAKE MEDICATION, you will need to have your doctor determine whether it is safe to take while breastfeeding. Gregory White, MD compiles a reference on drugs in breastfeeding, which is published as a supplement to the journal *Veterinary and Human Toxicology.* The 1984 edition appeared as the twenty-six page Supplement One to Volume 26. It summarizes drug information by brand and generic names, and has extensive references to the medical literature.

This supplement, titled "Breastfeeding and Drugs in Human Milk" is much better than the *Physician's Desk Reference,* and is available to your doctor through his medical library. You can also order it for less than five dollars from:

La Leche League International
9616 Minneapolis
Franklin Park, IL 60131
(312) 455-7730.

If you and your doctor decide the benefits of breastfeeding outweigh the potential risks of the medication you are taking, you will proceed with your breastfeeding. *Whenever possible, collect milk and nurse before you take doses of your medication so that the drug levels will be at their lowest in your milk.*

BREASTFEEDING COMPLICATIONS may require your doctor's help for a cure. We talked about **MASTITIS** a little bit in the last chapter. If you have fever and a red tender breast, you've got mastitis until proven otherwise. **SEE YOUR**

DOCTOR AT ONCE to see if you need antibiotics. You will also need frequent drainage (best done by your nursing baby) if you are to keep from developing a breast abscess.

A BREAST ABSCESS can occur if breast-feeding is suddenly stopped when mastitis is present. These require surgical drainage and are very rare, very painful, and very preventable: keep on nursing should mastitis occur in you!

THRUSH is a yeast infection that can give your baby a sore mouth and a diaper rash and you a red, cracked, painful nipple. If your baby has white "milk curds" inside his mouth that won't wipe off and your nipples are red and sore, you've both probably got thrush.

See your doctor right away, before things get worse. *Both you and your baby need to be treated or the thrush will keep coming back.* Your doctor will probably prescribe nystatin drops for your baby's mouth and nystatin creme for your nipples. If your baby has a diaper rash, nystatin creme will be used here also.

Yeast thrives in warm moist areas, so frequent changings with disposable diapers and air-drying of your nipples will speed healing. Have your sitter boil the bottle nipples she uses for feedings twenty minutes to destroy the yeast or buy new ones. Boil or discard teething rings or other toys your baby chews on. *Continue treatment for two weeks to prevent recurrence.*

TO BE SUCCESSFUL IN WORKING WITH YOUR DOCTOR keep your roles clearly in mind. The doctor is the medical expert, and by the time you finish reading this book you are probably the breastfeeding expert.

Work together as a team. Show your doctor this book if he is interested or if he seems to be advising things contradictory to my program. If problems arise, be a troubleshooter. Clarify your goals, regroup, and think about what could be causing the problem. Try to come up with a plan of action, and enlist your doctor's help if necessary.

WHEN IN DOUBT ABOUT YOUR BABY'S HEALTH, see your doctor at once. Follow his medical advice, and consider his child-rearing advice. With a good doctor on the team, you will overcome any medical problems that might hinder your breastfeeding success.

14

Happy Endings: Your Baby Leaves the Breast

When should your breastfeeding end? When you and your baby want it to. That might be when your baby is six months old, a year, or even two and a half years old. Every woman will set her own goals, and what is right for one nursing couple may not be right for another.

Breastfeeding success is never having to say "I wish it had lasted longer." With the techniques in this book, you will be able to enjoy the benefits of a breastfeeding experience as long as you want to.

YOU SHOULD CONSIDER *nutritional* and *behavioral factors* in deciding how long to nurse your baby. There are *three nutritional stages* through which breastfeeding becomes less and less important as a food source. Any woman who may want to breastfeed to her baby's first birthday and

133

beyond needs to know about the behavioral stages of breastfeeding, or she may find herself in some embarrassing situations.

One friend of mine never even considered breastfeeding because she remembered how, when she was ten years old, her fifteen month old brother ripped his mother's dress open in church to nurse. Another friend was similarly accosted by her eighteen month old daughter on the beach. The little girl pulled down her mother's bathing suit and latched on before a crowd of hundreds!

Such embarrassment shouldn't happen to you because you will know about the behavioral stages your baby gradually goes through, and will have plenty of time to teach him breastfeeding manners before he gets old enough to do anything rude or embarrassing.

NUTRITIONALLY, your breastfeeding baby goes through three stages: the liquid, transition, and regular food stages.

THE LIQUID STAGE is the first six months of a baby's life. During this period there's no need for foods other than breast milk or formula, and no need for other liquids. Babies in this age group don't have the coordination to chew and swallow "solids" yet, as anyone can attest who has tried to feed cereal to a one month old.

THE TRANSITION STAGE is from six months to a year of age. At this time the calories needed for growth exceeds the capabilities of even the most prolific breastfeeding mother. *Between six and twelve months of age your baby must learn how to chew and swallow other foods. This is as critical a transition for him as learning how to nurse was.*

CHECK YOUR BABY'S READINESS for "solids" every so often by offering him a spoonful of rice cereal. (Squirt a little breast milk into the bowl for easy mixing.) If he clenches down firmly after the first spoonful or two and refuses to participate further, he isn't ready yet.

Sooner or later, your baby will get the "hungry cat" look while others are eating. That's the time to start offering weaning foods seriously. Doctors recommend iron-fortified cereals first because they are easy to digest and because babies at this age often have mild iron deficiencies.

If your baby is not very interested in solids at six months, there's no need to force him yet. My kids became intensely interested in sampling other foods at about seven to eight months of age.

Some breastfeeding mothers will have plenty of milk to support good weight gain until their babies are eight or nine months old. But between eight and twelve months your baby must get serious about switching from a liquid diet to other foods.

DURING THE TRANSITION PERIOD, offer your baby other foods first when he seems hungry, and coordinate his feedings with regular meal times. At first he won't eat very much, but by a year he will be chowing down like the rest of you.

YOUR NUTRITIONAL STATUS may have some influence on how soon your baby needs to go onto transition foods. In third-world countries where mothers' diets are grossly inadequate, babies who don't get started on transition foods by the time they are six months of age end up smaller than their peers and are more likely to get sick.

You don't have to make major changes in your diet to breastfeed your baby successfully, because even the worst American diet is nutritionally superior to the diets in these third-world countries. Just eat your regular foods to satisfy your hunger.

If you want to clean up your act a little, increase fresh fruits, vegetables and protein sources, and cut back on junk foods with too much salt, sugar, fats, additives and empty calories. Calcium may be important, but don't go so enthused about whole milk and ice cream that your milk ducts get plugged up.

BOTTLE FIXATION doesn't have to occur in your breastfed baby, because bottles are not a major factor in his life. By nine months of age he will have enough coordination to handle a training cup with a lid. Your babysitter can begin to offer his breast milk or formula from a cup at this time, and he can start to explore juices from a cup, too.

DON'T FEED YOUR BABY SKIM MILK because it has too high a salt load and can make babies sick. Wait until his first birthday to begin feeding your baby whole or two percent milk.

ALLERGIES may be less frequent in babies fed only breast milk for the first six months of their lives. Until about six months of age, your baby's stomach and intestines are "leaky" and allow some foreign proteins from his food to be absorbed whole. These whole proteins may sensitize him to have more allergies later.

Your breast milk has no foreign proteins that might sensitize him, and by the time he is six months old his gastrointestinal tract has matured so that the proteins in his food are broken down and not absorbed whole.

If you or your husband's families have lots of allergies, hay fever, asthma, eczema or hives, the American Academy of Allergy recommends you try to totally breastfeed your baby until he is six months of age. This will not guarantee that he will never develop allergies, but it will improve the odds that he won't.

For nutritional reasons the American Academy of Pediatrics recommends all babies be breastfed if possible until one year of age. *But there's more to breastfeeding than just nutritional concerns. Nursing your child is an experience with many dimensions.*

NURSING IS THE BEST WAY to comfort an explorer who suddenly finds the world more than he can handle. It's an adventure that continually changes as your child grows and develops. And it is a way of communicating without words.

BREASTFEEDING MAKES YOU UNIQUE in your child's eyes. *Other people may feed him, change him, play with him and love him, but only you nurse your child, and this makes you very special to him.*

COMFORT AND COMMUNICATION become the primary reasons to continue breastfeeding beyond the nutritionally important first year of life. I think under natural circumstances most children would wean themselves between two and three years of age.

After the first year, nursing becomes more infrequent, but it can still be special to mother and child alike. As my daughter Susan got better at eating other foods, she took less at the breast and nursed fewer times a day. By the time she was a year old she was eating three meals a day like the rest of us, and the amount of milk I made dropped off quickly.

If Susan was more interested in playing than nursing when we got home in the afternoon, she played, and my milk production was scant enough that I was no longer uncomfortable going long periods with my breasts unemptied.

We quit comfort nursing in public between six and twelve months when a cracker and a hug started doing the job. We gradually cut down the length of our morning wake-up nursing sessions, and by the time she was a year old Susan was eating a big breakfast.

Until Susan was eighteen months of age, she counted on being nursed to sleep at night if I was home. By this time I was not interested in any long nursing sessions, and unless Susan had had a really bad day, we kept things brief.

Now at two and a half years of age she vaguely remembers what she used to do at the breast. Once every couple of weeks or so she will uncover my breasts as I change for bed. She may just grin, point, and cover me up again. If she does begin to nurse, it's just for a suck or two before she is off to other things again.

You should know about the behavioral stages of breastfeeding if you think you might want to continue breastfeeding past the first year of your baby's life.

THE FIRST BEHAVIORAL STAGE is what I call the *"Get the Baby and Feed Him"* stage. For the first four or five months, your baby can cry when he wants a meal, but he can't come and get it. You are clearly in control of the situation.

THE "BABY COMES TO YOU" STAGE is next. Over a period of several months your baby will get progressively better at coming to the source when he wants to nurse.

At first, your baby will not come unless he sees the breast. I used to bathe my babies as they sat on my lap in the tub, and about five months of age they got coordinated enough to turn around and latch on. So I learned how to bathe nursing babies.

As your baby learns to climb up in your lap, a new era begins, and it is most definitely time to start teaching him when and where you don't want him to nurse.

When he first starts climbing into your lap to nurse he'll be puzzled unless you show him the breast. It will take him at least two months to figure out that your breasts are somewhere behind your clothing, and another several months until he has the manual dexterity to undo your clothing to get to them.

Begin teaching your baby when and where not to ask for the breast while he is still puzzled and incapable of effective action so you don't end up embarrassed when he reaches his full capabilities.

WHEN YOUR BABY FINALLY LEARNS how to undress you to get to the breast, he has reached the *"Baby Comes to You And Can Have His Way With You"* stage. Now it is too late to teach him manners, so don't put off his education this long.

As he starts climbing into your lap when he wants to nurse, distract him with a toy if other people are present or you are in public. No one will notice what you are up to, and gradually your baby will learn that he doesn't get anywhere when other people are around.

Start doing other things during the day for comfort, like hugging without nursing or getting a drink of water. Make up for particularly bad days with a longer-than-usual bedtime nursing session.

You will probably have a few battles over whether to nurse or not as your baby gets older, but if you stand your ground you and your baby will soon learn to respect each other's limits, and can both continue to enjoy your special nursing relationship. *Recognition of each other as people is an important strategy for dealing with toddlers, regardless of whether you are still nursing or not.*

If you might like to experience nursing a toddler until he weans himself, teach him your limits as he grows so you won't be put in an uncomfortable nursing situation when he is older.

IF YOU WILL BE WEANING YOUR BABY before he weans himself, try to do so gradually over a period of weeks to months by gradually cutting out a feeding every week or two. I never recommend an abrupt stop to nursing if it can be avoided. It's traumatic to the baby, and will be uncomfortable to the mother if she is still making a lot of milk. It's much better for both of you to wean your baby slowly.

WHAT IF YOU CHANGE YOUR MIND after you have weaned your baby? What if you wean your baby and he develops allergies to all formulas and would do better on breast milk?

It is possible to start nursing again through a process called **RELACTATION.** The Lact-Aid we discussed in Chapter Twelve was actually developed for use by an adoptive mother who wanted to experience breastfeeding, and is used commonly by women who stopped breastfeeding and want to start again. Nipple stimulation for two to three hours a day will quickly build your milk supply up again, and the Lact-Aid allows your baby to get formula while giving you the necessary nipple stimulation.

HOW LONG YOU BREASTFEED depends entirely on you, your circumstances, and your desires. You might decide that three months is long enough, or your baby might finally say goodbye to the breast at three years of age.

As long as you meet your breastfeeding goals and are satisfied, you have been successful because you won't have to say, "I wish my breastfeeding had lasted longer."

Take some time now to decide what you want to do and write down your breastfeeding goals. Use this book as a coach, and review your goals in life frequently, especially if you get discouraged.

NINETY-FIVE PERCENT of all new mothers have the biological equipment necessary to breastfeed their babies successfully. Now that you have read this book you also have the knowledge that is critical for breastfeeding success. Good luck, and enjoy nursing your baby!

Afterward: Will You Let Me Know?

WILL YOU LET ME KNOW what you think of this book? I have written and rewritten it ten times, and each time it has gotten better. By now we think it is easy to read, entertaining and informative, and we hope you think so, too.

It would be impossible to include everything I know about breastfeeding in this book, and there is a lot I probably don't know about the subject. I am not the world's leading expert in this area, and I don't have all the answers to all the questions that could come up.

I do believe, however, that this introduction to breastfeeding has the core material working mothers need to successfully breastfeed, and that ninety-five percent of all women who use these methods will reach their breastfeeding goals.

If you have further questions or special needs, books listed in the bibliography can provide you with additional information. Health care workers who deal with breastfeeding mothers should obtain one of the books written for health professionals.

I WOULD APPRECIATE any comments you can make about this book, especially if you seem to have had more than your fair share of problems.

How can I make this book better? What should I include that I didn't? What should I leave out or clarify further? What did you like best about this book? What did you like least about it?

How long did you breastfeed your baby? How long had you wanted to breastfeed? Was this your first baby or first breastfeeding experience?

What other breastfeeding information did you get, and from what source did it come? How does this book compare to other information you have seen about breastfeeding?

Would you buy this book for a friend? Do you think your co-workers who are expecting babies should read it? Can you recommend this book for other working mothers?

THANK YOU for the opportunity to share my interest and enthusiasm for breastfeeding with you and your family. May you have as much fun with breastfeeding your baby as I have had with mine. And when your breastfeeding experience is over, will you let me know?

Glossary

afterbirth cramps. Mild uterine contractions after childbirth as the uterus returns to its normal size. Nursing a baby speeds up this process.

aroela (a-REE-o-la). The dark-skinned area surrounding the nipple under which the important milk sacs lie. In most women it extends an inch or so from the nipple. In other women this darker coloration may cover half the breast.

behavioral milestones. A list of activities such as sitting up, rolling over, and picking up a raisin used by pediatricians to see if babies are developing properly.

bottle fixation. Where a baby becomes so attached to the bottle that she won't give it up as she gets older. Three-year olds in the supermarket sucking on baby bottles have bottle fixation.

colostrum (co-LA-strum). The milk secreted for a few days after childbirth. It has a deep yellow color and is rich in infection-preventing antibodies. Babies are born with thick sticky dark *meconium* (me-CONE-e-um) stools which are sometimes hard to pass without colostrum's laxative effect.

engorgement. Where the breasts, aroelae, and nipples become swollen, tender, and firm. This occurred frequently when babies were kept in a central nursery and brought to their mothers only every four to six hours to nurse. It won't happen if your baby is nursed every couple of hours for the first couple of weeks. If the nipples and aroelae become too firm, one may need to massage them and manually express some milk before the baby can latch on.

145

expression, manual. Where the mother squeezes breast milk out of the breast. Its success depends on stimulating let-down via the nipple nerves and effective compression of the milk sacs under the aroela. It is useful in several situations: to save milk for the baby to drink later, to begin the flow of milk before the baby takes a sore nipple, to have the most vigorous part of let-down finished before a baby who chokes easily takes the breast, and to motivate a lazy baby to take the breast.

hospice. The original definition was "a house of shelter or rest for pilgrims." The modern hospice movement provides support to cancer patients and their families, often with a place to stay other than the hospital when they are too sick to stay home.

impotence. 1. Being totally unable to perform some task, being without bodily strength or lacking in power and ability. 2. When a person (usually a man) can't perform sexually. 3. Feeling powerless. 4. Breastfeeding impotence is the feeling that you can't successfully breastfeed your baby.

inverted nipple. Where the nipple does not stand out but is hidden back in the breast. Inverted nipples can be drawn out by suction as when a baby takes the breast or by gently squeezing over the line where the dark-skinned aroela meets the rest of the breast. *Women with inverted nipples can definitely nurse their babies -- it may just take a little more practice and patience than otherwise.*

lactation. The process whereby milk is made in the breasts. This normally occurs after a pregnancy as a baby's nursing stimulates production of prolactin hormone, but it can occur in other circumstances. *induced lactation* is where a women who has not just had a child gets enough nipple stimulation to make milk and nurse a child. Anthropologist Margaret Mead reported cases of aunts and grandmothers, some of whom had never even been pregnant, breastfeeding babies whose mothers died in childbirth. *relactation* is where a mother who stopped breastfeeding starts it up again.

La Leche League. Founded in 1956 by breastfeeding mothers to provide information and support to other mothers wanting to nurse their babies, it is now an international organization with over 4,000 La Leche League groups in forty-three countries. "La Leche" is Spanish for "the milk." The League distributes many books and pamphlets on breastfeeding topics, and probably has a local chapter near you. See page 130 for the League's address and phone number. Call them if you are interested in contacting the local group nearest you.

maintenance calories. The amount of food required to provide fuel for maintaining your weight and carrying out your activities. In addition to maintenance needs, children must have additional calories to grow.

membranes, ruptured. Membranes are the "bag of waters" that surrounds a baby before birth. Sometimes these spontaneously rupture at the onset of labor, and the baby is usually born within twenty-four hours after rupture.

milliequivalents. A term used in chemistry for measuring numbers of charged particles such as sodium or potassium.

nose breathing. Newborn babies are obligate nasal breathers, meaning that they must breathe through their noses. They learn as they get older how to breathe through their mouths.

pacifiers. Devices used to quiet babies by letting them suck on something. The fact that bottle-feeding parents often think pacifiers are essential reflects the strength of babies suckling needs. Breastfeeding mothers should avoid the use of pacifiers so their babies' suckling needs can stimulate a plentiful milk supply. *If God had meant babies to have pacifiers, they would be born with pacifiers in their mouths!*

puberty. the transition stage from childhood into sexual maturity. *breastfeeding puberty* is the transition stage from non-lactation to lactation.

sleep-wake cycles. The daily pattern of sleepiness and wakefullness. Disordered cycles can cause insomnia and daytime sleepiness, and are best treated by delaying bedtime two to three hours each night until sleepy at bedtime.

Sudden Infant Death Syndrome (also known as "crib death"). The sudden unexpected death of a young infant who had been apparently well or had suffered from only trifiling signs of disease. SIDS accounts for one fourth of infant deaths between the ages of ten days and two years. SIDS is the cause of death of over 25,000 infants in the United States each year, and is the leading cause of death in infants between one month and one year of age.

Most infants die in their sleep and are found dead in the early morning hours; relatively few collapse while someone is in attendance. One third of SIDS babies were premature. The cause of SIDS remains unknown despite intensive research efforts over the last decade. Some studies have shown a decreased incidence of SIDS deaths in breastfed compared to bottle-fed babies. Other research supports the premise that infants are less likely to die of SIDS if they sleep near other people than if they are put in an isolated room by themselves at night.

xylocaine. A pain-killing agent used by physicians and dentists to provide anesthesia for painful procedures such as pulling teeth or sewing up cuts. It works by blocking nerve receptors in the local area to which it is applied. With the receptors blocked, no nerve impulses are sent, so no pain or other sensations are felt.

Bibliography

For General Reading:

Applebaum, Richard, MD. *Abreast of the Times*. 1983. (ISBN 0-686-87525-7). La Leche League.

Brewster, Dorothy P. *You Can Breastfeed Your Baby Even in Special Situations*. 1979. (ISBN 0-87857-276-7). Rodale Press Inc.

Eiger, Marvin, MD and Olds, Sally. *The Complete Book of Breastfeeding*. 1973. (ISBN 0-553-23419-6). Bantam.

Ewy, Donna and Ewy, Roger. *Preparation for Breastfeeding*. 1983. (ISBN 0-451-12485-5). NAL.

Gerard, Alice. *Please Breastfeed Your Baby*. 1970. (ISBN 0-451-11605-4). NAL.

Keith, Donald, eds. *Breastfeeding Twins, Triplets and Quadruplets: 195 Practical Hints for Success*. 1982. (ISBN 0-932254-02-0). Ctr Multiple Birth.

Kippley, Sheila. *Breastfeeding and Natural Child Spacing: The Ecology of Natural Mothering*. 1975. (ISBN 0-14-003992-9). Penguin.

Kitzinger, Sheila. *The Experience of Breastfeeding*. 1980. (ISBN 0-14-005591-6). Penguin.

La Leche League. *The Womanly Art of Breastfeeding, 3rd ed*. 1981. (ISBN 0-912500-11-5). La Leche League.

Messenger, Marie. *The Breastfeeding Book*. 1982. (ISBN 0-442-26577-8). Van Nos Reinhold.

Mitchell, Ingrid. *Breastfeeding Together*. 1975. (ISBN 0-8164-9351-0). Seabury Press.

Nursing Mother's Council of the Boston Association for Childbirth Education. *Breastfeeding Your Baby, 2nd Edition.* 1981. (ISBN 0-89529-141-X). Avery Pub.

Pryor, Karen. *Nursing Your Baby.* 1973. (ISBN 0-06-013443-7). Harper-Row.

Raphael, Dana, PhD. *The Tender Gift: Breastfeeding.* 1976. (ISBN 0-8052-0519-5). Schocken.

Thevenin, Tine. *The Family Bed.* 1976. (ISBN 0-960-2010-1-7). Thevenin.

For Health-Care Professionals:

Childbirth Education Association of Greater Philadelphia, Inc. *Counselling the Nursing Mother.* 1983. (ISBN 0-89529-206-8). Avery Pub.

Food and Nutrition Board, National Research Council. *A Selected Annotated Bibliography on Breast Feeding 1970-1977.* 1978. (ISBN 0-309-02796-9). Natl Acad.

Goldberg, Larry and Leahy, Joann. *The Doctor's Guide to Medication During Pregnancy and Lactation.* 1984. (ISBN 0-688-02792-X). Morrow.

Goldfarb, Johanna, MD and Tibbetts, Edith. *Breastfeeding Handbook: A Practical Reference for Physicians, Nurses and Other Health Professionals.* 1980. (ISBN 0-89490-030-7). Enslow Pubs.

Helsing, Elisabet and King, F. *Breastfeeding in Practice: A Manual for Health Care Workers.* 1982. (ISBN 0-19-261298-0). Oxford U Pr.

Jelliffe, Derrick, MD and Jelliffe, E. F. *Human Milk in the Modern World: Psychosocial, Nutritional and Economic Significance.* 1981. (ISBN 0-19-264921-3). Oxford U.

Lawrence, Ruth. *Breast Feeding: A Guide for the Medical Professions.* 1979. (ISBN 0-8016-2897-0). Mosby.

Rice, Ilene, PHN. *Breastfeeding, A Heartstart.* 1983. (ISBN 0-912825-00-6). Heartstart.

White, Gregory, MD and White, Mary. *Breastfeeding and Drugs in Human Milk.* 1984. (ISBN 0-686-87532-X).

Index

151

About The Author

Music lover, gardener, physician and parent, Marilyn Grams grew up in Gillette, Wyoming, the granddaughter of pioneer homesteaders. Showing her independence at an early age, she turned down college scholarships to study computer programming at a business school in Denver.

Following a stint as a computer programmer at Walter Reed Army Hospital in Washington, D.C., she attended the University of Missouri in Columbia, majoring in music and graduating Summa Cum Laude in 1974.

She and her husband attended the University of Utah School of Medicine in Salt Lake City on Navy scholarships. After rotating internships in Sioux Falls, South Dakota, they completed their Internal Medicine training at San Diego Naval Hospital, where their daughters were born.

After completing their military service with the Marines at Camp Lejeune, North Carolina, they moved back to the mountains of Wyoming, where Dr. Grams now directs an Ambulatory Care program for adults.

About This Book

This book is a blend of high-tech production methods and a very high-touch subject. The manuscript was written and revised on an Apple Macintosh computer using Apple's *MacWrite* word processing software.

Page composition and lay-out was performed on the Macintosh using *ReadySetGo,* an interactive page makeup program developed by Manhattan Graphics, 163 Varick Street, New York City, NY 10013, (212) 989-6442.

Typesetting was done on an Apple *LaserWriter* printer.

Book manufacturing was performed by McNaughton & Gunn Lithographers, Ann Arbor, MI 48106.

Share Breastfeeding Success
with a friend or co-worker. If someone you know has a new baby or is expecting, let us send them a brochure about this book. (We'll not mention your name.)

Please send brochures about this book to:

Name:_____

Address:_____

City:_____State:____ZIP:_____

Name:_____

Address:_____

City:_____State:____ZIP:_____

Name:_____

Address:_____

City:_____State:____ZIP:_____

Please send this letter to:
Achievement Press
P. O. Box 608
Sheridan, WY 82801

Thank you!

ORDER FORM

Yes! I'd like my own copy. Please send _____ copies of Breastfeeding Success to:

Name:_____

Address:_____

City:_____State:_____ZIP:_____

Please send a gift-wrapped copy to:

Name:_____

Address:_____

City:_____State:_____ZIP:_____

Gift card to read: _____
Order additional copies on a plain sheet of paper.

Buy three books and get one free:
We pay shipping and sales taxes!
     1 book send $15
     2 books send $30
     4 books (one free) send $45
Enclosed is a check or money order for $_____.
Send To:
     Achievement Press
     P. O. Box 608
     Sheridan, WY 82801

All Books Guaranteed:
If not completely satisfied return this book with your receipt for an immediate full refund.

Share Breastfeeding Success
with a friend or co-worker. If someone you know has a new baby or is expecting, let us send them a brochure about this book. (We'll not mention your name.)

Please send brochures about this book to:

Name:_____

Address:_____

City:_____State:_____ZIP:_____

Name:_____

Address:_____

City:_____State:_____ZIP:_____

Name:_____

Address:_____

City:_____State:_____ZIP:_____

Please send this letter to:
Achievement Press
P. O. Box 608
Sheridan, WY 82801

Thank you!

ORDER FORM

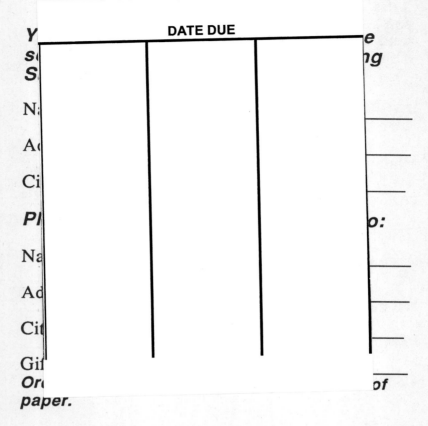

DATE DUE

Y...   *e*
s...   *ng*
S...

N...

A...

Ci...

Pl...   *o:*

Na...

Ad...

Cit...

Gif...
Or...   *of*
paper.

Buy three books and get one free:
We pay shipping and sales taxes!
     1 book send $15
     2 books send $30
     4 books (one free) send $45
Enclosed is a check or money order for $_____.
Send To:

     Achievement Press
     P. O. Box 608
     Sheridan, WY 82801

All Books Guaranteed:
If not completely satisfied return this book with
your receipt for an immediate full refund.